the view from mars

daylen, kai & seth larsen

For Jacqueline, the mom and wife we always
wanted.

CHAPTER ONE,

or "THAT TIME MOM SAT US DOWN ON THE COUCH"

"...the weather will be amazing." -
MOM

My name is Mars. From the moment I entered this world, about thirteen years ago, life has been a continuous realization of how much better things would be if my name was Troy or Brock, or literally any other name.

But it's like many wise people have told me over the years: "Welp."

One more thing: I know this font looks strange, and there may be occasional blotches or whiteout. That's because I'm using an old typewriter-- which I'd never recommend, by the way-- but there's a reason for it, and I'll get to it shortly.

For now, I'll start at the point where everything changed. It was last summer, on a mundane Friday morning, just six weeks before I graduated from sixth grade. I was daydreaming of riding my bike to the lake.

Mom yelled at us from the hallway.

"Everyone, get on the couch!"

Generally, Mom is great. If it weren't for her, I wouldn't know that there's a right and wrong way to fold hand towels. But gathering us on the couch was unusual, and I was immediately suspicious.

"Don't you think this is odd?" I asked my sister Barrie.

"What's odd," she responded, "is an integer that's not a multiple of two."

"Huh?"

"A number that, when divided by two, is a fraction."

I stared blankly, before offering, "No big words in the morning, okay? We talked about this."

Barrie isn't your normal ten-year-old. She's tall and thin and wears glasses, but the thing to know about her is that she reads books that

don't even fit on bookshelves, and
knows a lot more than I do even though
she's two grades behind me.

Once, when she was a toddler,
Mom read to her, "Twinkle, twinkle,
little star, how I wonder what you
are?" Barrie thoughtfully replied, "A
luminous, gaseous spheroidal body of
great mass that produces energy
through nuclear fusion reactions."

Someday, she'll perform a heart
transplant for an endangered elephant,
while I'll still be trying to figure
out whether you're supposed to say
"all of the sudden" or "all of a
sudden."

I shoved my seven-year-old
brother Sumo to the couch. Everyone
has always called him that—— they
don't know that's not his actual name.
I don't even think *he* knows. My dad
gave him the nickname when he was a
baby because of his thick thighs. Mom
asserted that it was "insulting to
Japanese culture," but then she
started calling him that, too.

"I'm allowed," she argued. "I'm
Asian."

Technically, she's Chinese, not
Japanese...but apparently that covers

3

her. Since I'm half-Asian, I guess I'm allowed, too.

Anyway, when Sumo stood up on the couch, I knew what was coming next. He pulled off his boxers, scratched his belly, and proudly surveyed the living room.

Approximately fifty percent of being Sumo's brother is seeing him naked, but from different rooms in the house.

Meanwhile, I looked at the clock and started worrying. That's my special gift. Superman got Kryptonite, the Tyrannosaurus rex got little baby arms, and I got worrying. Or, as Mom calls it, "crippling anxiety."

My fear of being late isn't just paranoia. It began in kindergarten. One day, my dad dropped me off to school late. Unfortunately, the class had already left on a field trip.

I spent the day alone in a classroom with a giant stuffed peep-- those yellow marshmallow Easter bunnies-- except this was a life-sized one. Its eyes followed me wherever I went, and I'm pretty sure it even winked at me at one point...which also explains my intense fear of peeps.

4

To this day, Mom gives my dad a hard time about leaving me in that classroom alone.

I should mention that my dad hasn't lived with us for over a year now. I'm not suggesting it was the result of that incident, I'm just saying that it didn't help.

Anyway, once we were all on the couch, Mom looked us over.

"I have some news," she began. "I've accepted a new job."

She paused to study our reactions.

"The job is in Los Angeles...which is where we'll move once school ends."

Um-- what was that?

"Isn't that exciting?" Mom asked, optimistically.

"Not really," proclaimed Sumo. He didn't get that she wasn't looking for a response.

Barrie crinkled her nose: "Why can't you just keep the job you already have?"

Mom took Barrie's hand, as if she'd rehearsed for this question. "This could be the fresh start we need."

Fresh start from what? I wondered.

"What about Dad?" I demanded.

"He won't be joining us. Not at first, anyway," she articulated.

(Let me pause to note that my parents are separated. Don't say they're divorced, or Mom will correct you very quickly. She still wears her wedding ring, too. It all makes sense in her head-- it's just that the rest of us aren't allowed inside it.)

Barrie folded her arms: "Why do *you* get to decide?"

"That's what mothers have to do," Mom declared.

Wrong, I thought. *Moms have to yell at us about cleaning our rooms and taking too long in the shower-- they do NOT have to move the family across the country.*

"What if we move to Los Angeles, and there's a seismic event?" Barrie challenged.

"Yeah," I jumped in, just before realizing I had no idea what that meant.

"We can't move," I protested. "I love it here in Ohio."

Okay, that wasn't exactly true, but I was certain I didn't want to move to the other side of the country.

"You'll make new friends," Mom offered, "and the weather will be amazing."

The weather? We sat in silence.

"We'll have lots more conversations about it, okay? But now that the cat's out of the bag, let's get to school," Mom directed.

Sumo then wanted to know which cat was being kept in a bag, and why someone could be so cruel as to do that. He tends to miss the main idea.

Mom pulled me aside.

"It's time," she stressed.

"For what?"

"For you to step up this summer and be a leader for Barrie and Sumo."

"I don't want to be that."

"That's not how life works."

"You never asked what *I* wanted."

"They need you to tell them it'll be okay."

"Will it?"

She pushed us out the door, and I think I spent the rest of the summer trying to get that question answered.

I began to stew, because I have a black belt in that.

If there's a real or imagined person I most relate to, it's Bruce Wayne. Sure, he tends to dwell on things, but you can't deny his confidence, wealth, and mastery of all martial arts.

I may not be confident or rich, but I also don't have any fighting skills. What I'm saying is, I dwell on things.

For instance, I lie awake at night contemplating whether I'm doing enough to stop another *Smurfs* movie from happening.

I'm even still trying to come up with the perfect comeback for Keith, that annoying kid in my class, when he smirked, "What planet are you from, Mars?"

That was two years ago, in fourth grade. So, yeah, I think about things way too much, and I never actually *do* anything.

9

That evening, I wrote an online review of California. Not a restaurant in California...I mean, the entire state.

"Zero out of five stars," I wrote. "Many earthquakes. Would not recommend."

That'll teach California, I thought.

The one thing I knew was that we couldn't prevent a move to California unless we found a way to get our parents back together.

That meant I'd have to *do* something.

But what?

CHAPTER TWO,

or "THAT TIME THAT I GOT A TYPEWRITER"

"It's not that simple, son." - DAD

"Someone wants to talk to you," Mom advised, as she handed me her phone.

I held the phone to my ear.

"Hey, bud."

I was happy to hear my dad's voice, because it had been a while.

"There's a Reds game tonight. You guys want to join me?" he proposed.

One thing to know is that my dad is a sportswriter. He goes to baseball games and writes about what happened. Mom thinks he got into that because he doesn't like to talk to people. As for me, I don't know why someone would read about it when they could just flip on the TV and watch the highlights, but that's what he does.

11

Dad used to be a great athlete, too. He could've been a professional ball player, he likes to tell us, until he injured his knee.

As for my parents' relationship, there were happier times. Barrie determined those times to be 73 percent happier.

There was the time we went to the State Fair and got free rides on the Ferris wheel until Sumo puked. My parents held hands the whole time, and we ate ice cream sandwiches.

That was a good day.

But in recent years, there were arguments behind closed doors. Both my parents kept those kinds of things to themselves. They said it's something that a lot of marriages go through, and that it wasn't my fault, and that they hoped to be together again at some point.

My thing is this: if kids have to work things out, then adults should, too. Martin Luther King, Jr. said that, I believe.

All I knew was that we'd seen Dad less and less.

I agreed right away to go the

12

ball game. Barrie and Sumo did, too.
We conspired that maybe Dad could help
us stop the move to California.

I was ready for the game two
hours early with my cap and glove. If
Dad came early, I was going to be
ready.

In the front driveway, we played
handball against the garage to pass
time. If there's one thing I hate,
it's playing handball with Sumo.
(Okay, I also hate world hunger and
stepping on Legos while barefoot-- so
I guess that's three things.)

Predictably, when Sumo lost to
Barrie, he kicked the ball over the
fence in protest, so it only made
sense that I pinned him down until he
cried and Mom yelled at me.

Basically, if blood, sweat and
tears were not shed, did we even play
handball?

Honestly, that's true about most
activities we do as a family.

As we sat on the curb waiting
for Dad, Barrie determined that the
likelihood of him showing up was less
than twenty percent.

"He's just running late," I

shrugged. "Probably got a flat tire."

Dad's cars have always been their own form of adventure. Mom calls them—— well, I'm not allowed to say what Mom calls them. He buys cheap used ones, refuses to get them fixed, and drives them until they die a slow, painful death. Then he blames the car.

We laughed as we recalled the car with a taped bumper and windows that you couldn't roll down.

There was one car that even Dad hated so much that eventually he threw the keys into a river, only to discover that he'd accidentally thrown someone else's keys from a completely different car.

That was a thing that happened.

Then there was the car with the floor rotted out. Dad put wood boards in place of the floor to keep us from falling through. Mom called that one the "clown car"—— that's one name I'm allowed to say.

The clown car was the last car Dad had while he still lived with us. I know that because we usually measured our childhood not in years, but based on which car Dad was driving at the time.

Mom came out with a radio.

"What's that for?" I asked.

"To listen to the ballgame while you wait."

"I don't want to ruin it."

"Okay. Well, it'll be there."

As the sun went down, Barrie went inside to read. Sumo and I turned on the radio for an update. The Reds had an early lead. We high-fived, but Sumo's enthusiasm quickly wore off and he went inside, too.

"He'll be here any minute," I called after him.

I threw the tennis ball against the garage, testing out my new curveball. Mom didn't even complain about the loud thud the ball made against the garage door.

I started thinking, again, about comebacks for Keith from two years ago.

What planet am I from? I'm from the planet with no gravity-- which means you can't hold me down.

Oooh, burn! I thought. *That's*

the one. Then I realized I'd need to explain the joke, and before I'd be able to finish informing Keith how funny it was, he would've pantsed me.

I kept an eye out for Dad's car. I wasn't sure what car he was driving these days, so I paid particular attention to ugly cars that sputtered. Each one that passed brought a renewed hope, until I realized that it, too, wasn't his.

Each time I had to go to the bathroom, I hurried back in case Dad arrived while I was gone.

On the radio, the fourth inning turned to the sixth. The Reds lead had faded, and so did my expectation that Dad was coming.

Finally, I grabbed the radio and went inside. Mom opened my bedroom door.

"Hey, Mars, you okay?"

"The bugs were getting to me."

"Bugs?"

"Yeah."

"Listen, I'm sorry your father didn't show up. He hasn't been very dependable."

"I'm sure something came up."

Mom sighed as she stood in my doorway.

"Mars, he's been battling a problem."

"What do you mean?"

"Drinking."

"You mean, like, beer?"

"He's working on it, but it's still a problem for him. It's time you knew that."

"All right."

"I'm sorry, Mars. If you're upset, or--"

"No."

"You sure?"

"Uh-huh."

"If you wanna talk..."

I didn't. She kissed me on the forehead.

Later, I walked out to the living room to watch TV, because I wanted to stop thinking about what Mom had told me.

I nodded off on the couch, when suddenly I heard a knock. One of those late-night talk shows was playing on the TV by then, so I knew it was late.

There was Dad, in the doorway, under the porch light. He looked tired, and his shirt was rumpled.

He didn't say anything at first. Then he handed me an old typewriter. He explained that he'd used it as a kid, and his father had used it before that. He described how, when he was my age, he would listen to ballgames and boxing matches on the radio and write about them on this typewriter. Then he'd compare what he wrote to the article in the next morning's newspaper.

I remembered playing with his
typewriter years ago, but the keys
always got stuck.

"I had the ink replaced, and
fixed a couple of the keys. I thought
you might like to bring it with you to
California," he said.

"What would I use a typewriter
for? Computers are way better."

"Maybe write about your life,"
he suggested.

I wasn't sure I wanted to do
that. My life isn't all that
interesting.

"Who'd want to read about it?"

"I would," he answered. "I'd
read it."

19

I set the typewriter down on the floor, because it was getting heavy.

"Can't you stop Mom from taking us to California?" I posed.

"I'm afraid not, bud."

"Don't you want to come with us?"

He looked down at the floor. "It's not that simple, son."

I wanted to tell him that I was hurt and angry that I'd sat on the curb for hours, waiting for him. And I wanted to ask him if what Mom said about his drinking was true.

Like usual, I just couldn't do it.

"Dad," I began, "Why didn't you come get us for the game?"

"I'm...having a hard time right now."

He cleared his throat, and then he brushed my hair out of my face.

"I'm sorry," he said, voice cracking.

"About what?"

"All of it. Everything."

He trudged back to his car--
which was as junky as the rest of his
past cars. The engine puttered.

He looked at me through the
windshield, nodded, and gave a sad
smile.

And then he was gone.

I replay that memory a lot in my
head, even now.

CHAPTER THREE,

or "THAT TIME I FACED A BEAR"

"Don't you smell that fresh air?" -
MOM

"Do not argue. About anything. Ever."

That was the instruction Mom gave us just before we began our cross-country trip.

"When you say never," began Barrie, "do you mean the duration of the trip?"

"No. I mean forever."

Despite the number of motivational speeches where Mom said, "With your talents, there's nothing you can't do," there certainly seemed like LOTS of things we couldn't do-- and arguing topped the list.

While we travelled through
Kansas City, Sumo complained he had to
pee. Mom encouraged him to hold it
until we got to a truck stop-- and by
"encouraged," I mean threatened.

She eventually pulled over and
told him to pee by the side of the
freeway.

Instead of trying to shield
himself, he took his pants off right
out in the open.

"Get your pants on!" Mom yelled.

We watched the horrified eyes of
the passing drivers as they saw the

23

bare butt of a kid happily spelling his name in the dirt with his urine, admiring his work.

Upon further inspection, he'd actually managed to write his name quite legibly.

As we drove through New Mexico, Mom had the idea of staying overnight at a campsite. She thought it was a good opportunity to sleep under the stars.

"Don't you smell that fresh air?" she asked, as she inhaled deeply. "It's free, just like all the best things in life."

Well, some of the worst things are free, too, I grumbled to myself. *Like, when you hold the door open for someone and then realize there are dozens of people right behind that first person, so you're left holding the door for hours? That's also free.*

I've never understood the point of camping. I mean, I get it if this was the Gold Rush, and we were miners headed west on a wagon. But if you have an option, why would you choose to sleep outside on purpose?

There are two types of people in this world: those who enjoy camping,

24

and smart people. When you have the opportunity to sleep on a bed, you take it. Every time.

The more I thought about sleeping outside, I thought about mosquitos. Ants. Spiders. Coyotes. But mainly wolves.

I know it's been stated that "there's nothing to fear but fear itself," but I disagree. There are lots of things to fear, and many of them can be found while camping.

We got a little fire going, where we made noodles for dinner and s'mores for dessert. It seemed like maybe this camping thing wasn't so bad...but then the night happened.

When we all went to bed, I couldn't sleep because Sumo was snoring his head off. I was miserable.

Finally, after I fell asleep briefly, I felt a weird sensation and opened my eyes-- and saw a bear standing over me. I don't mean an analogy, as in life is hard and it feels like a bear is hovering over you. I mean, like, *an actual bear.*

There are many situations you can prepare for in life. But laying there, with a bear staring at you face-to-face, is not one of them.

Do I move? Do I not move? I **was** terrified.

After what seemed like a century, I heard the loud banging of a pot.

It was Mom, trying to get the bear's attention. The bear tilted its head and looked at her, wondering why this little woman was not afraid of it.

She suddenly threw one of the pots, and hit it right on the nose. It was a really good throw, as a matter of fact. Then she threw a second one, and hit it on the head.

You know those nature movies
where the bear gets up on its hind
legs and lets out a roar that can be
heard from another solar system?

Well, this bear didn't do that.

It just sort of raised its
eyebrows, shrugged, and walked away.
Maybe it figured there were plenty of
other campsites that didn't have a
crazy woman throwing pots.

The bottom line was that Mom
saved my life. You would have never
known that she was frightened, too--
but she swears she was.

I would've hugged her in
appreciation right away, but it was an
hour before I could move...and my
first move was to change my underwear.

After that ordeal, we continued
making progress toward California. A
couple of days later, we came upon the
Grand Canyon. Since I'm afraid of
heights, it didn't seem like a good
fit for me.

There were endless possibilities
of misfortune that could visit us.

Like, *what if I randomly decided
I needed to jump across it? What if I
gave my legs a stretch, prepared*

myself, ran as fast as I possibly could, but then I was only able to jump five feet of literally the three miles needed to make it to the other side?

And what if the last thing I saw while falling was Sumo and Barrie looking down from the edge of the canyon, asking why I'd tried to make the jump in the first place? I'd have no answer. What then?

Mom had to drag me out of the van to even get a view of it.

"It's just a huge hole in the ground. What's the big deal?" I argued.

Sumo desperately wanted to throw a rock down the Grand Canyon. Mom told him no, but he did it anyway.

Barrie noted, "It'll hit the bottom in six seconds."

We counted down the seconds... five, four, three, two, one--

"Hey!" hollered some guy from the bottom of the canyon, who evidently didn't appreciate Sumo's effort. On the other hand, Barrie's calculations were impressive.

Even though I wasn't close to the edge, I never let go of my mom while looking at the canyon. I have to admit, it was beautiful the way the setting sun bounced off of the red rock. It made me feel like a tiny part of a big planet.

"We're moving to California!" I shouted into the Grand Canyon.

I listened for the echo, and I could swear it answered back, "Terrible idea!"

The next day, while we drove through Nevada, there was one point where Barrie and Sumo were asleep. I was staring at the passing desert--the barren land, baked by the relentless sun.

I began thinking about comebacks for Keith from fourth grade. Again.

What planet am I from? I'm from the planet that revolves around awesomeness.

No, too childish.

Suddenly, I heard sniffling. I thought I'd imagined it until I saw tears rolling down Mom's cheeks through the rearview mirror.

I'm sure she thought I was asleep. I realized in that moment that she'd been strong for all of us during this whole time, but nobody was there for her.

I don't know exactly why she was crying, and she wouldn't want me to know that she was, but I felt really bad for her.

I wanted to say something-- anything at all-- to make her feel a little better, but nothing came to mind. So, I did what I always seemed to do: nothing.

I still regret that.

CHAPTER FOUR,

or "THAT TIME I ALMOST ATTEMPTED 'THE SWEEPER'"

"I have to see this." - CHUY

"So, here it is, guys," Mom declared, as we arrived at the parking lot of an apartment complex. "Our new home."

There were a few tough-looking guys huddled together. One of them wasn't wearing a shirt so that he could show off a tattoo across his stomach that declared, 'Only God Can Judge Me.'

I feel like Mom probably judged him, though.

Ironically, she was the one who instructed me to not judge a book by its cover-- but I never struggled with that concept. For example, the covers on the math and science books at school always had kids laughing and smiling, and I never felt that way about those subjects. No one did,

31

except maybe Barrie.

The street was lined with palm trees, which I'd only ever seen in movies before. An ice cream truck stopped on the street corner, as kids gathered around it.

We spotted the apartment manager. Stating the obvious, Sumo marveled, "Oooh! He's smoking!"

"Never smoke," Mom commanded. "There's a seventy-five percent chance you'll die."

"You're saying, then, if I smoke, there's a twenty-five percent chance I'll live forever?" Barrie retorted.

It was a good point, truth be told-- so good that Mom just glared at her.

Unfortunately, the apartment manager heard Sumo.

"I'm not smoking," he grumbled. "I'm playing a small flute."

Once he put out his cigarette, he walked us to our new apartment. There were two bedrooms.

My mom claimed the bigger room for Barrie and herself. I let her slide, since she's an adult, and also gave birth to me and everything.

Sumo and I got the smaller bedroom. He complained about the injustice, and sighed heavily as if he was weighed down by all the problems in the world. He emphasized how small the room was by "accidentally" bumping into the walls and throwing his hands in the air in protest.

Mom looked out the window in the living room.

"Hey! We have a view of the swimming pool from here."

Wait, what was this? We excitedly gathered around the window. Sure enough, in the middle of the patio area was a swimming pool.

The only problem was, there was no water in it-- which is generally an important aspect of a pool. Our enthusiasm deflated liked a shriveling balloon.

"That's on the list of things to fix," the apartment manager grunted.

"How long has it been on the list?"

He thought for a moment: "About six years."

I was getting the impression he didn't like us very much.

As we dragged our boxes from the van to our apartment, I noticed a group of kids *skateboarding* in the pool. I'd never seen anything like it.

Some of them were doing fancy tricks. Mom was frustrated because I was distracted by the skateboarders instead of helping her move stuff-- but I was still doing a lot more than Sumo, who was completely useless.

Finally, when we were almost done, Mom told me, "Why don't you just take a break and make some new friends?"

I grabbed my skateboard from one of the boxes in my room. It was an old birthday gift from my grandmother, and I wasn't even sure if the wheels still worked.

"What do you think you're doing?" Mom scrutinized.

"Bringing my skateboard."

"You're not skateboarding in that pool."

34

That wasn't a problem, because I wasn't about to try. I just wanted it to appear that I "might" skateboard.

As I strolled over to the group of kids, I put on my shades to look cool, just like they do in movies-- except in my case, no building spontaneously exploded in the background.

These kids look really tough, I thought. *I'm one of the only kids not wearing a hooded sweatshirt. Why are they even wearing hoods? It's got to be ninety degrees out here. Maybe it's some socially accepted article of clothing they wear. Like, everyone just knows. And they now know that I'm not from here. I'm a fake, a fraud. I hate California. I wish we'd never--*

"Hey, bro," nodded the smallest kid. "You're the new family in apartment 34?"

I looked at him and considered the various possible responses, before carefully selecting the one that sounded the toughest: "Yes, that's correct."

"I'm Chuy," he remarked, pronouncing it like "chewy."

35

Out of all the kids, he was the one that talked the most, despite his lack of size. Nobody seemed to pay him much attention, but that didn't stop him. I don't think his mouth ever quit moving.

He pointed at my skateboard and called it an "old-school board," and I didn't know if that was a good thing or not. Then he shook an inhaler before breathing it in deeply. I would soon learn that he couldn't go anywhere without it.

"What's this dude doing here?" a huge kid in an orange shirt asked.

I felt a little sorry for whatever dude he was talking about.

That was right around the time
that I realized, by process of
elimination, he was talking about me.

As I looked around, I was
suddenly very aware that I was the
only kid in the crowd that wasn't
Latino. (Also, the fact that he was
staring at me was a clue.)

Back in Ohio, they called me the
"Asian kid." Here, it looked like I
was going to be the "white kid."
Either way, I got the sinking feeling
I didn't belong.

Luckily for me, Chuy saved me by
changing the subject.

"What's your best trick?" he
pried.

I had to think for a minute,
because sitting on a skateboard and
rolling down a driveway didn't seem
like the right answer.

I could feel the kids staring at
me. I saw a broom nearby, and
vocalized the first word that came to
mind. "The, uh... sweeper."

I thought that would be the end
of it. Instead, everyone's jaws
dropped. It turned out that the
sweeper is an actual trick, and with

my luck, these guys knew exactly what
it was. As a matter of fact, I was
probably the *only* one who didn't know.

"I guess Danger's your middle
name," Chuy commented.

"Actually, it's Fitzgerald," I
responded, pausing to allow the crowd
to break out in appreciative laughter.

The laughter that I foresaw did
not occur. Instead, actual crickets
chirped.

"Right. Well, I have to see
this," Chuy observed as he handed me a
helmet.

I'd never worn a helmet before,
so I joked, "Helmets are for girls."

One of the kids stepped forward,
wearing a hooded sweatshirt.

Once the hood was pulled down,
it revealed the face of a girl. I was
not expecting that.

"This is my cousin Izzie," Chuy
noted. "She lives next door to me.
She's the only one who can do the
sweeper. Well, along with you now."

I wasn't sure if kids in Los
Angeles do high-fives, or handshakes,

or fist-bumps...so I just nodded
toward her.

All of the chaos swirling around
us turned to meaningless noise as she
came into focus, and I realized how
pretty she was.

*Maybe this was the girl I was
destined to meet,* I thought. *Maybe we
have a lot in common, and we'll start
hanging out all the time, and we'll go
to the school dance and it'll be
amazing.*

*Then again, what if we go to the
school dance, and she's practically a
professional dancer? Like, what if
she's really good at the same dances
that Mom tried to teach me once-- the
ones where I kept accidentally*

39

stepping on her feet?

I'll still have to see this girl all the time, and I'll have to come up with really awkward small talk about the weather and my thoughts on, like, climate change.

Then I remembered that my mom instructed me that I'm not into girls anyway, because I need to focus on school.

Izzie snapped on her helmet, and suddenly dropped down the side of the pool, swerving side to side, circling around the pool. As all the kids watched, she picked up speed-- going faster and faster. I was shocked at how skilled she was.

Darting around the pool like a fireball, she completed a spin move and then launched herself out of the pool, grabbing the skateboard in mid-air as she landed on her feet.

I couldn't believe what I'd just seen. So, naturally, I pretended I'd seen it a million times before.

"She just hit us with the sweeper!" Chuy pointed out.

I nodded, as if I knew.

Izzie took off her helmet and flipped it to me.

"You're next," she offered.

Everyone formed a semi-circle around me, waiting in anticipation.

Chuy suggested, "When you launch out of the pool, try to land on your hands. I saw that on TV once."

"You mean like on one hand?" I asked, trying to picture what he was talking about.

"Whoa! You can land on one hand? That's even more insane than the guy on TV! I *have* to see this," Chuy expressed, buzzing with excitement as he snapped Izzie's helmet on my head.

I had to do something. So, I secretly unscrewed one of the wheels of my skateboard until it fell off.

"Aw, man," I apologized. "Sorry, guys. Next time."

The wheel kept rolling until it landed at the feet of the biggest one, the Kid With the Orange Shirt.

"Use mine," he challenged, as he handed me his board.

41

That completely foiled my plan. It hadn't occurred to me that everyone there had a skateboard, and any one of them could've easily lent me one.

I had no Plan B.

The kids lined up along the pool to chant, "Sweeper! Sweeper!"

I positioned myself on the skateboard at the edge of the pool. Staring at the bottom of the pool, I identified the section where I was most likely to crash on impact.

I thought to myself, *Look, am I the best athlete in the world? No. But can I rise to the occasion? Also, no. But could I at least pretend to be brave? Still, no.*

"Go!" directed the Kid With the Orange Shirt.

"What are you, chicken?" mocked someone else.

Izzie watched me expectantly, hand on her hip.

I remembered my Dad telling me, "Don't be afraid to fail," but I just don't think he was aware back then of the number of times that would happen.

42

I was frozen in fear. I couldn't budge. I silently prayed for a way out of this-- or at least that my heart and other organs be put to good use after I'm gone.

What happened next was a blur. Someone grabbed me by the collar and yanked.

"I said no skateboarding!"

It was Mom, and she was furious. The crowd of kids grumbled, knowing their chance to see me go down in flames had vanished.

I pleaded with her, half-heartedly. Don't get me wrong...it was really embarrassing, and I knew instantly that I'd never be able to downplay this.

But the truth is, this was less embarrassing than literally perishing in front of everyone, which is what would've happened if she hadn't intervened.

So, more than anything, I was grateful. Sometimes, prayers get answered.

CHAPTER FIVE,

or "THAT TIME I THOUGHT I SHOULD FIGHT FOR BARRIE'S HONOR"

"So, what are you gonna do about it?"

- THE KID WITH THE ORANGE SHIRT

On Mom's first day in her new job, she gave me a long speech about looking after my siblings until she could get back home on her lunch break.

"With great power comes great responsibility," she explained.

I knew I was getting a lot of responsibility dumped on me, but where was this great power? I didn't see it.

I did my best to manage Barrie and Sumo, but when Barrie asked if she could play in the patio near the pool, I told her it was okay. Mostly, I just wanted to get rid of her.

I probably should've watched her
more closely, but I was enjoying the
freedom of not hearing her theories
about, well, everything.

It wasn't, however, *completely*
quiet, because Sumo was singing some
song from the radio at the top of his
lungs in a never-ending loop, but at
least he couldn't get underneath
Barrie's skin, so I didn't have to
break up any arguments.

I sprawled out across the couch
and treated myself to a second bowl of
cereal. Life was good...for about
three minutes.

I never got to finish that second
bowl, because Barrie came flying
through the door, crying and pointing
to a scraped knee.

In between sobs, she claimed there
was a kid that wouldn't let her play.
He had pushed her, causing her to trip
and fall.

Look, I'll be the first to tell you that my sister can be really annoying, but I'm the only one who's allowed to feel that way.

Before I could even think straight, I ran out to the patio.

"Who pushed my sister?" I demanded.

I even tried to make my voice sound deeper, but really it just made my voice crack.

I looked around. I only saw one kid in the patio. It was the Kid With the Orange Shirt from the group of skateboarders. Because of course it was.

Unfortunately, my sister had not mentioned that her nemesis was built like a refrigerator, and about that size.

"I did," he confirmed without hesitation.

My heart sank. I wondered how many teeth was the appropriate amount to lose over this issue.

I tried to give him any possible opportunity to end the conflict, hoping he'd take it.

"Well, I'm sure it was an accident."

"Accident? Nah."

"Or some kind of miscommunication."

"Nope."

"Maybe you tripped, and put your hands out by mistake to regain your balance, which then bumped my sister."

"No. So, what are you gonna do about it?" he sneered.

Probably nothing, and then run? I thought to myself.

I considered explaining to him that next time, it would be most appreciated if he could be a little more considerate, as long as he was okay with it.

But just then, Chuy walked by, and I devised a plan. In a flash, I grabbed Chuy and pull him toward me.

"Don't hold me back!" I told him.

I pretended that Chuy was the only person or thing preventing me from teaching the Kid With the Orange Shirt a lesson he'd never forget.

"Let me go!" I instructed Chuy, while at the same time holding onto him with a death-grip, practically begging him to save me.

Chuy was completely baffled.

The Kid With the Orange Shirt was equally perplexed as he watched this go on. Finally, he shoved Chuy away.

"Well? He's not in your way anymore."

"Oh," I answered.

"I don't like you. Or your family."

His eyes darkened, menacingly, as he waited for me to respond.

"I'm...I'm sorry you feel that way."

I don't think he expected that reply.

"Wanna know why I don't like you?"

I really didn't, as a matter of fact.

"You don't belong," he continued. "You shouldn't have moved here."

"Is it because I'm white? It is, isn't it? I'm Asian, too, you know. Like, half. So."

He put up his hands in a boxing stance. It didn't seem to help that I was half-Asian.

"Come on, then, Bruce Lee," he provoked.

That's when I saw into the open door of my apartment, and my eyes locked onto Barrie's. She was looking at me like I was her only hope in this cold world.

Well, maybe it wasn't that dramatic, but that's what it felt like. I took a deep breath.

From there, things went downhill quickly.

The Kid With the Orange Shirt punched me in the stomach.

"Fight back!" he demanded.

There are over seven billion people in the world, and none of them were going to save me from what was about to happen.

I remember Chuy saying, "Leave him alone!" and I'm pretty sure I caught a

glimpse of the Kid With the Orange
Shirt charging toward me like a
hurricane-- or maybe a whirlwind. I'd
have to look up the definitions in
order to determine which natural
disaster it most resembled.

In any case, there was a lot of
activity, and all of it was directed
at me. I think Chuy tried to pull him
off of me at one point, but the
evidence suggested he didn't have much
success.

For what it's worth, I would not
recommend getting beaten up. It's
overrated.

I remember hoping that maybe this
was one of those gang initiations,
where you have to get beat up in order
to join. Maybe I was in a gang now?
That would at least be one positive
out of the situation.

I only know that when I regained
consciousness, I was lying on my back
and looking up at my sister and Sumo
standing over me. It appeared that I
was still not in a gang.

Sumo wasn't wearing any pants, of
course, but at least he had the
decency to wear boxers. Chuy helped me
to my feet.

"I'm sorry that happened, Mars," Barrie remarked, which didn't really help my aching face feel any better.

I was embarrassed that I couldn't protect her, and that she had to see me like that.

I'd like to think that we all silently agreed to never speak of this incident again.

Later, Mom pressed me to describe the boy who hit me. "Angry," I noted.

That may have not been what she meant, but at least she didn't ask me anymore questions.

That night, I lay awake. Why did the Kid With the Orange Shirt dislike me so much? What did I do to him? I couldn't understand. I now hated California even more, if that was possible.

More importantly, why was I so fearful to do anything? I knew Dad would be humiliated if he had seen that. I was sick of living inside my own head. Sick of being a pushover.

I wished that I could have a nickel for every time I didn't have the guts to do something. I'd still be the same fearful kid, but at least I'd have a ton of spending money.

No one is ever going to do that to me again, I vowed. *Next time, I will not just stand there and do nothing,* I told myself over and over.

But what? What would I do next time?

I kept replaying that scene in my mind.

"Mars, are you okay?" Sumo asked.

It startled me. I thought he was asleep. I hadn't even realized I'd been crying.

"Yeah, I'm fine," I told him, and I couldn't even convince myself.

CHAPTER SIX,

or "THAT TIME SUMO WAS THE FINAL VOTE"

"Can we keep him?" — *BARRIE*

"If it was zero degrees outside yesterday, and today it's twice as cold, how many degrees is it?" asked Barrie.

"No, I meant questions about *what to do while I'm gone*," Mom sighed.

"Oh. Then, no."

I could tell Barrie was getting depressed. I was not thrilled with living in Los Angeles either, but she *really* wasn't.

I wasn't exactly sure why she was so miserable. She didn't even have lots of friends back in Ohio. In fact, she only really had one, a girl named Janelle who-- not to be mean-- but I'm pretty sure couldn't speak. At least,

54

I never heard her say a word in my life. The two of them would sit next to each other and read books.

Barrie was always so freakishly smart that none of the other kids on the school playground knew what to make of her. Sometimes I felt bad for her because I knew she wanted more friends, but I couldn't really blame the other kids, either.

And at least she couldn't have been as lonely as the guy who invented the boomerang-- that guy must have had some serious problems finding friends.

One Tuesday morning, after Mom left for work, I heard Barrie crying. It was more of a quiet sniffle, but I knew. I should've asked her what was wrong, but I was never good at stuff like that.

I did, however, take her to the park with Sumo, and that's where things took an interesting turn.

Near the playground, a scrawny little dog started following her around. It was dirty and mangy, and needed a haircut. It also had a strange way of walking-- it preferred to use its front paws to drag itself along. It didn't even have a collar.

The other thing was that it looked a lot like Boomer, the dog we had back in Ohio years ago. Dad had found Boomer on the side of the road one day and brought him home. From that point, I spent a lot of time playing with him, up until he got sick and died.

From the moment we arrived at the park, this dog wouldn't leave Barrie's side.

"Can we keep him?" Barrie petitioned.

As the leader of the kids, I had to put my foot down: "No way."

The real reason for my stance was that Boomer's death was right around the time things started to fall apart between my parents, and that was not something I wanted to be reminded of every time I saw this dog.

Barrie wanted to name it, but there was no way I was falling for that. Once you name a dog, it becomes yours. That's the rule.

But she went behind my back. When Mom got home, Barrie wove a story about how special this dog was-- and blah, blah, blah.

To hear Barrie tell it, you would've thought this dog could fold laundry, wash the car, and bring about world peace. She performed a big song and dance, and the only thing missing was the jazz hands.

Mom finally remarked that we had to decide together-- the three of us kids.

I glared at Mom. *How could she fall for this? What happened to me being the unquestioned leader of the kids?*

It turns out that when your younger sister tells your mother that she's sad, everything goes out the window.

I huddled with Barrie and Sumo for a quick vote. Of course, I voted no and Barrie voted yes. While I viewed this stray dog as a reminder of the past, Barrie seemed to view it as a clean start for the future.

That left Sumo as the deciding vote, a frightening thought.

Realizing that he now controlled our fate, he began to milk the situation. He rubbed his chin and paced the floor, loving all the attention-- exactly how he likes it.

"Well?" I demanded.

"Still thinking," he responded.

We waited. And waited.

Only after I opened our bedroom door to yell for Mom did he finally say, "Okay. Wait. I need to talk with each of you so you can convince me of your side."

He couldn't be serious! Except he was. I saw what I was up against-- all Barrie needed to do was put together another Oscar-winning performance, and it would sway Sumo's vote.

I knew what had to be done. I pulled Sumo aside.

"We can't keep this dog."

"Why?"

"I'll give you two reasons," I stated, as I handed him two crisp dollar bills.

It crushed me to reward Sumo, and I felt bad for stooping so low just to block Barrie from getting this dog, but sometimes a man's got to do what a man's got to do.

"I'll think about it," Sumo commented.

I just gave him two bucks, and he still needs to think about it?

It made me angry that he just wanted me to sweat it out, but I knew he'd do the right thing-- otherwise he was going to get pounded.

While I vacuumed the apartment, the dog barked non-stop. *Oh, great,* I thought, *we'll be safe if a vacuum cleaner ever tried to break into our place.*

When we gathered as a family, I had to pretend I didn't know how Sumo was going to vote. I nibbled my fingernails and tapped my toes nervously. I thought it was a great performance...maybe even as good as Barrie's.

Sumo stepped forward. "I've thought about the good things and the bad things about owning a dog," Sumo narrated.

"And my decision is..."

As he pretended to make up his mind, I thought about things I could say to cheer up Barrie, who would surely be disappointed about having to give up her new furry friend.

I'll tell her that this dog would just make us sad because it'd remind us of Boomer and the fact that our parents weren't together anymore, so in the end, this really is for the best.

Then Sumo announced his decision.

"We'll keep the dog."

What. Just. Happened?

Barrie hugged him in
celebration.

My anger boiled...until I was
struck by a thought.

*Maybe I underestimated Sumo.
Maybe he thought it was more important
to be a supportive brother in Barrie's
time of need than pocketing some money
from me. I mean, I'll still pound him
mercilessly, but I might feel bad
about it. What had I done-- bribing my
little brother? Maybe I got what I
deserved.*

Later that night, as Sumo and I
lay in our beds, I told him, "I
thought we had a deal."

"We did," Sumo responded, "but
Barrie gave me three bucks."

So, after all that, I hadn't
underestimated how weak Sumo was. I'd
only underestimated the amount it took
to buy his vote.

"You better sleep with one eye
open," I threatened.

And he did. In the middle of the

night when I got up to pee, I saw one of his eyes staring at me nervously.

The next day, we had another family discussion about the dog. This time, it was to name him.

I suggested "Three Dollar Dog," but no one liked that, for some reason.

"I've got it," Barrie announced.

(Before I disclose her decision, and to make a long story even longer, let me point out that Barrie's very favorite mathematician is someone named Lisa Jeffrey, who-- as Barrie likes to tell us-- used "symplectic geometry to provide rigorous proofs of results in quantum field theory." Or something like that.

Now that you know this, we can return to the action.)

"I'd like to name the dog Jeff."

We thought she was kidding, but she was insistent that the name honor her favorite mathematician. And since the dog was male, Jeff would have to do.

Later, when the three of us kids took Jeff for his first walk, I thought about Dad.

"I wish he were here to meet our new dog," I sighed as we waited for a street light to turn green.

"Let's print a photo of Jeff and send it to him in the mail!" Sumo suggested.

It wasn't a terrible idea.

"We could pretend it was Mom who sent it!" he added.

Now we're onto something! I thought. *Maybe that's just the thing to get them talking again.*

I immediately forgave Sumo, mentally, for siding with Barrie in the vote to keep Jeff.

"It might make him feel like he's more of a part of things," I responded.

"But Mom wouldn't write a letter. Nobody does. She'd just compose an email," Barrie said.

Sometimes she can really halt enthusiasm with facts and figures and stuff.

"Well, maybe the computer isn't

working," I posed, in air quotes.

"He'd still know it's not her handwriting," she argued.

That made me think of the typewriter Dad gave me.

Sumo and Barrie guarded my bedroom door as I quietly brought the typewriter out of its box in the closet.

I slipped a piece of paper into it, and pounded my fingers on the keys as if I were some newspaper journalist from World War I. Each key I hit responded with a loud 'clack.' I was surprised that the ink really did seem to work.

I gave a thumbs-up to Barrie and Sumo, and then wrote a short letter to Dad. I explained that we got a new dog that looked like Boomer, and I added that we missed him. I signed it as Mom.

The next day, we dropped it off in the mail and hoped for the best.

CHAPTER SEVEN,

or "THAT TIME I ALMOST DIED"

"Have you ever wanted to get on a train and just go till it ends?" - *IZZIE*

"Let's go to the beach!" Chuy urged. "We've got a few boogie boards."

This was one of the first times I'd hung out with Chuy and Izzie, so it was especially important that they not think I was uncool.

Izzie agreed it was a great idea, but both of them noticed my hesitance.

"You coming?" Chuy asked.

"Uh, I can't," I said.

"Why?"

There were so many reasons that I didn't know which one to go with.

65

"My mom," I said.

"She won't let you go to the beach?" Izzie questioned. The tone of her voice made realize my plan to not look uncool wasn't succeeding.

"We can take the Metro and be back by the afternoon," she said. "Your mom would never know."

"What if there are sharks in the ocean?" I asked.

The second reason, of course, was that the idea of the ocean frightened me.

"No sharks, bro," said Chuy. "They don't come close to the shore."

He's lying, I thought. *He didn't mention the ferocious lion-sharks.*

Most people don't believe that lion-sharks exist, but I'm completely convinced they do. I've read about them on the internet.

Wouldn't it be my luck to be the first person ever attacked by one?

What if I get attacked by a bunch of them? I wouldn't even know what to call them. Would it be a SCHOOL of lion-sharks? Or a PRIDE of

66

lion-sharks? It's confusing.

I moved onto my next excuse,
which was really my primary reason for
not going.

"I don't have enough time. I'd
have to be back by three o'clock."

Since I didn't have many friends
in Los Angeles yet, and didn't have
much to do, I knew that the mailman
came to our apartment complex around
that time on Saturdays.

This mattered because I was
expecting a letter back from Dad any
day, and I couldn't take the risk that
Mom would intercept it and realize
we'd pretended to be her. If she found
out, it would ruin everything.

But Chuy and Izzie surprised me.
They said we could be back before
then.

Chuy tossed me a bathing suit to
borrow, and I'd run out of excuses.

But if I'd been able to watch a
trailer for what would transpire,
there is no way I'd have gone.

Here's how it unfolded.

We skateboarded to the Metro Rail station, bought our tickets, and went through the turnstile. But just as the doors on the Metro began to close, we realized we were on the wrong one.

I barely made it out before the doors slammed shut. Unfortunately, the boogie board I borrowed didn't make it-- the door closed on my hands as the Metro took off, and I dropped it.

At least Izzie was there to offer encouragement--

"You lost the best board!" she griped.

Well, maybe not.

"It's okay," Chuy shrugged. "It was old, anyway."

After we got on the correct
Metro, Izzie sat down beside me. This
made me nervous.

*Think of something to talk
about. Something interesting,* I
thought.

I determined that my opening
remark had to be between 8-22 words.
She'd think I was awkward if it was
less than that, but annoying if it was
more.

"Did you know that a ten-gallon
hat actually only holds three-quarters
of a gallon? So misleading," I
blurted.

That was not my best work.

"First time on a Metro?" she
queried.

I nodded.

"One day, I'll travel the entire
country," she announced.

"To go where?"

"Far away."

I squinted in confusion.

"I've never gone anywhere," she

69

commented. "Haven't you ever wanted to get on a train and just go till it ends?"

"And then what?"

"See new things. That's the point."

"I have not wanted to do that."

"You lived in Ohio. What's that like?"

Note: I could've described the rolling hills and country roads, or the factories and farmlands. In real life, though, I said:

"It's okay, I guess."

Obviously, I'm not "Mr. Personality," and I may not be "super confident," but at least I know how to "use quotation marks."

We got to our stop and exited with our boogie boards-- well, except for the one I lost, which was being enjoyed by some lucky kid, miles away in downtown.

As seagulls circled, we walked past a pier with an arcade and a Ferris wheel.

"I wish I had some money for the arcade," I commented.

"That pier is one of my favorite places in the world," Izzie observed.

"Which games do you play?"

"None."

"What do you do, then?"

"I just watch people."

"What's so interesting about people?"

"It takes your mind off of things. Seems like that'd be good for you."

Great, I thought, *she already knows I think too much. Stop thinking!*

I contemplated that for a while.

We trudged through the hot sand, and staked out a spot on the beach. Chuy found a seashell.

"Look, guys," he noted, "if you hold this to your ear, you can hear the ocean."

That reminded me of the time my dad suggested that if I held my ear to

71

his wallet, you could hear a sigh of despair from his bank account.

"What time is it?" I asked.

"You're already worried about the time?" Izzie chastised.

But they couldn't have possibly understood the importance of getting back home before the mailman.

Chuy checked his waterproof watch. "We have a few hours. No problem!"

Chuy and Izzie raced out into the water first, laughing all the way. After some encouragement, they got me into the ocean.

Izzie showed me how to paddle on the board, and most importantly, how

to use it as a lifesaver if I found
myself in the middle of the ocean.

When it was just Chuy and I in
the water, he caught me by surprise.

"Do you like Izzie?"

Chuy has this way of saying
exactly what he's thinking. It's
weird-- I have no idea how you would
go about doing that.

I hesitated.

"I'm serious, bro. I just wanna
know," he asserted.

I mumbled and shook my head.

"I'm just saying that I get it,
if you did like her," he insisted.

"Well, that's good to know," I
replied. "I mean, if I did like her--
which I don't. She's cool, I guess.
But I don't like her like that."

He nodded. Then I casually
added, "Why? Did she say anything
about me?"

"Nope," he answered.

I couldn't hide my
disappointment.

73

"See? I can tell you like her,"
Chuy laughed.

The waves were getting bigger by
then. I caught a glimpse of one that
was, unquestionably, the largest wave
of all time.

Was this a tsunami? Maybe it was
the fury of Neptune, the Greek god of
the sea I'd read about in class.

Whatever it was, it was headed
straight for us-- and me in
particular, as if it identified me
from far away and declared, "This
specific kid needs to be taught a
lesson."

I started paddling, as if my
flailing arms and legs were going to
get me anywhere.

Might as well just wait for it,
I thought. Whatever was going to
happen, I wasn't going to stop it.

I thought about the best way to
divide my life savings-- which, in
truth, is basically just a pile of
used t-shirts.

I said a quick prayer to
apologize for eating Barrie's
Halloween candy two years ago and
blaming Sumo for it. If I was going to

die here, I wanted to go out with a
clear conscience.

I wondered if Mom would be okay.
I thought about Dad-- how was he doing
back in Ohio? Did he miss us?

Then I wondered who would speak
at my funeral, and what would they
say?

*What if my P.E. teacher stood up
and told everyone I couldn't even do
five pull-ups?*

Meanwhile, the Ocean Wall of
Death prepared to unleash its rage.

My life flashed before my eyes.
Sadly, it was a brief flash, because I
really haven't done a whole lot with
my life so far.

Goodbye, cruel world.

Whoomph.

I was hurled down toward the
ocean floor, and everything went
black.

Silence.

Am I dead? I remember thinking.
*Did I just die? Because if I died,
I'll be very disappointed that I never*

did respond to Keith from fourth grade.

The next thing I knew, I was dragged to shore by a lifeguard on the beach.

I wasn't certain how long I'd been unconscious.

"You're okay, bro," Chuy insisted.

"How big was that wave?"

"I don't know."

"Twenty or thirty feet high, right?"

"Uh, couple feet, I guess."

I looked around, expecting to see carnage and mayhem all along the beach. I only saw kids building sand castles, laughing and playing.

How could I have been the only one affected by this monstrous wave?

Suddenly, I remembered the mailman.

"What time is it?" I panicked.

Chuy looked at his watch.

"We should get going," he conceded.

My face turned pale. I mean, I couldn't see my face, but I know it was. I badgered Chuy until he admitted it was two o'clock.

We did the math in our heads as we raced to the Metro.

"If everything goes right, we'll get there at exactly three o'clock," Chuy said as he huffed and puffed.

Once we were on the Metro, I stared at Chuy's watch as each second ticked off.

"Staring at it isn't going to help," Izzie reminded, rather unhelpfully.

I pictured Mom finding a letter from Dad-- and the punishment that would follow.

Once we got to our stop, we jumped out of the Metro. We estimated that it was a ten-minute run, which was a problem because it was 2:52 by that point.

I saw the mailman's truck drive past.

No!

I took off running as hard as I could, lungs burning. Izzie ran alongside me-- effortlessly-- but Chuy had difficulty keeping up.

"What's the hurry?" he called after us.

When I turned the corner toward our apartment complex, my heart pounded as I saw the parked mailman's truck.

Maybe I can catch him before he puts the mail in our slot, I thought.

I raced to Chuy's apartment to throw on my regular clothes, then I sprinted toward the mailboxes-- until I had to stop dead in my tracks.

It was the Kid With the Orange Shirt walking in my direction.

Why now, of all times?

I didn't know if he saw me, but I ducked and ran the other direction. I had to run all the way around the complex to get to the mailboxes from the other side.

Once I got there, I discovered Mom chatting with the mailman. Even worse, she was already holding the mail.

I gingerly approached, until she paused.

"Mars, do you need something?"

"What? No. I'm fine."

She nodded and kept talking. Studying the small stack of mail in her hands, I spotted something.

A letter.

It looked like it was from Dad.

Had she seen it? I was frantic.

"Mom, I can take the mail to the apartment," I suggested.

"That's okay," she answered.

Does she know?

When she finished her conversation, I followed her into the apartment and desperately watched her sit down to open the mail.

I sweated as she opened up the first envelope.

It was a bill of some kind.

79

She skimmed it, muttering, then reached for the next piece.

I held my breath.

But it, too, was another bill.

I felt like I was walking the plank, and there was nothing I could do about it.

Then I saw it-- Dad's letter at the top of the stack. *Do something!*

"Hey, Mom?" I began.

"What?"

"Why did the guy who wrote the Star-Spangled Banner say "o'er the ramparts we watched" instead of "over the ramparts"?

It was the best I could come up with in a moment's notice.

Mom looked at me and frowned.

"What are ramparts, anyway?" I added, "and why were we watching them? I have so many questions about this."

It seemed that Mom was considerably less curious about these concerns than I was.

Suddenly, there was a loud bang.
And then crying.

Sumo had flipped off the couch and
hit his head on the coffee table.

Mom jumped from the table to help.
It was a terrible sight-- his head
bleeding on the carpet.

On the other hand, there was Dad's
letter sitting on the table, free and
clear. Life sometimes presents
interesting choices.

I'm not an awful person. I'm truly
not. Don't judge me until you've
walked a mile in my shoes.

Actually, it's best that you don't
walk a mile in my shoes. You'd just be
tired, and I'd probably want my shoes
back.

The point is, it was the
situation that dictated my next move.

In the middle of the chaos, I
grabbed Dad's letter and snuck it to
the bathroom to read it without Mom
knowing.

It was a handwritten note. He
mentioned he liked the photo, and
agreed that Jeff looked like Boomer.
He said he hoped we'd visit him in

Ohio soon. Then he concluded that he was glad we were getting some use out of his old typewriter.

It felt good to hear from him.

I shared it with Barrie and Sumo, and we all agreed we'd write him back.

"We should *hand-deliver* the next one," Barrie posed.

I wasn't so sure. It seemed like a lot of work, especially when you could just spend fifty cents on a stamp and let the post office take care of it.

"It'd be great to visit him, wouldn't it?" she added. "In Ohio?"

I mean, I also tend to think it'd be great if I could ever fully understand when to use "whom" instead of "who," but some things are unlikely to happen.

But that didn't stop us from daydreaming about it.

CHAPTER EIGHT,

or "THAT TIME WHEN A WALK LED TO A
RUN"

"Get off of my phone!" ▬ *MOM*

Nearly every day during that
summer, Sumo and I joined Barrie to
take Jeff for a walk.

You could say it was a time of
bonding for all of us. That wouldn't
be entirely accurate, but you could at
least say it.

One particular morning, however,
Barrie insisted that she walk Jeff
alone. I knew she was still depressed
about the move to Los Angeles, so I
wanted to give her some space.

Walking Jeff usually took half an
hour, so I started getting a sick
feeling in my stomach about 33 minutes
after she left.

As each second ticked off, the normally imperceptible "chk...chk...chk" noise from the wall clock suddenly became much louder in my head.

I paced in circles, thinking about all the things that could've happened to her. I began to wonder if Barrie really could've gone to Ohio to deliver Dad a letter.

She's way too sensible to do something like that, I concluded.

Mom called from work to check in, and she could tell right away that I sounded a bit off. It's like a sixth sense moms have.

"Everything's okay?" she probed.

"What? Uh, sure. Yeah."

"Really? Because you're acting very..."

"What?"

"Strange."

"Wh-what do you mean?"

It's been said that there are times when you can feel your mom's glare through the phone. Well, I don't

know if it's been said, but I'm saying
it now-- because this was one of those
times.

The rest of the conversation was
basically her trying to get me to
admit that something was wrong, but I
held firm.

When we hung up, though, I knew
she'd be over soon to investigate.
Time was running out. I prayed that
Barrie would walk through the door
with Jeff, and all would be fine.

In the next instant, I heard the
keys jingling outside the door, and
Mom walked in.

"Mom. You're home early."

"I thought I'd take an early
lunch."

Act normal. Just act normal, I
thought. I grabbed a newspaper from
the coffee table and pretended to
calmly read it.

"Having trouble reading?" she
examined.

"Huh?"

"Your newspaper is upside down."

"Oh."

Sumo walked into the living room.

"Hi, Mom."

"Put some clothes on."

Sumo grumbled, as Mom turned her attention back to me.

"You let him just walk around like that?"

"He likes it."

"Where's Barrie?"

"Barrie?"

"Yes. Your sister?"

"Oh," I said casually, "She was reading a book. Then she took Jeff for a walk."

Mom leaned forward.

"What did you say?"

"Uh, she was reading a book...?"

"No, that last part. You said she took Jeff for a walk."

"Yeah."

"By herself?"

"I believe so."

"You...*believe* so?"

"Mm-hmm."

Mom was silent for a moment.

Maybe she's okay with it, I
thought. *Maybe she agrees that I was
being a good big brother, teaching her
responsibility, and--*

"You let Barrie walk Jeff *by
herself?!*"

"Well, yeah."

"When?!"

"When what?"

"When did she leave?!"

I looked at the clock, trying to
do the math in my head.

"Two hours ago," Sumo asserted.

Mom's face twisted in horror.

"No!" I replied defensively.
"Like, an hour and forty minutes,
tops."

This did not seem to calm Mom's nerves. She had us immediately trace the steps we always took on our walk with Jeff, forward and backward, but we couldn't find Barrie.

Mom called the police to file a Missing Person report.

I waited with Mom by the phone for what seemed like hours. By contrast, Sumo began to draw.

"Sumo," I scolded, "now's not the time for art."

"I'm making a poster."

"A poster? Why?"

"To help find Barrie."

Actually, that wasn't such a bad idea.

"Have you seen her?" the poster petitioned. "She's really smart." It included an arrow pointing to a stick figure that represented Barrie.

In Sumo's mind, I suppose, someone could recognize Barrie from the drawing. It didn't leave any contact information, so I guess he thought whoever found her would also automatically know where we lived and what our phone number was.

But at least he was trying to help.

Mom and I stared at the phone, as if concentrated focus would make it ring with good news. I didn't even want to blink, because if I did, it might break up the momentum we were building.

I considered disclosing to Mom that Barrie might be headed for Ohio. I debated whether I should tell her about the letters. I knew there would be grave consequences for me if I did, but this was Barrie's safety we were talking about.

Suddenly, the silence was shattered by the ring of the phone. We all jumped.

"Hello?" answered Mom, anxiously.

Sumo and I put our ears inches from the phone so we could hear the voice on the other end.

"Hi. I'm calling on behalf of the Los Angeles Education Foundation. How would you like to support our schools?" inquired a friendly man.

He could not have possibly known

what he'd just walked into.

"I'd love to," Mom began.

"Great."

Unfortunately for him, Mom continued.

"And I will do that at any time that is not THIS EXACT MOMENT."

"I see. Perhaps you could commit to a small donation of--"

"Get off of my phone!" Mom yelled at the man on the other line, before slamming down the phone practically through the receiver.

Sumo and I dared not breathe after that, at least for a few minutes. It was then that I unwisely decided to make conversation.

"That education foundation seemed like a worthy cause," I suggested.

Mom didn't respond, so I went on.

"Maybe in the future we should consider--"

"Mars?" Mom interrupted, "No."

That was a word I understood.

I needed to pee. As each minute ticked off, the urge became greater. It was as if little daggers were twisting into my bladder, one by one-- each one sharper than the last.

I couldn't leave the phone. If I did, I would miss the update.

Finally, I ran to the bathroom a second before I exploded. That was, of course, the moment we got another call.

This time, it *was* the police.

Barrie had been located in Nevada. She was on a train, headed for Ohio.

We raced to Union Station and waited several hours for her to arrive.

Finally, her train came. She exited with Jeff, and we immediately celebrated.

But then came the questions.

"Why?"

That's what we wanted to know.

"You're usually so much...smarter than to try and run away," Mom said.

I was paranoid Barrie was going to admit to Mom about the letters we'd exchanged with Dad, so I tried to make eye contact with her to plead with her not to do that.

But she didn't notice-- instead, she looked down at the floor.

"I missed Dad," she said. "I missed home."

I felt sorry for her, but I just didn't know what to do or say.

Mom hugged her, and then Sumo hugged her leg. It seemed like I should get in on that, too, but there wasn't much left of Barrie to hug.

"This is our home now, Barrie," Mom reinforced.

It didn't feel that way, though, and it didn't seem like it ever would.

On the drive home, I whispered to Barrie, "Why didn't you tell me you were going to do that?"

"You would've said not to."

"Yeah, because it was an awful

idea."

"At least I'm trying to get Mom
and Dad back together. What are you
doing to help?"

That was a knife in my back.

But she was right.

Barrie and Sumo were doing
things. I was supposed to be leading
them, and all I ever did was *think*
about doing things.

"Don't tell Mom about the
letters," I requested.

"She's going to find out."

"But it'll ruin things between Mom
and Dad."

"Things are already ruined."

"We need time to figure out how to
tell Mom about everything."

Thankfully, she agreed to stay
quiet for the time being.

Later that night, Barrie explained
to all of us how she'd gone to Union
Station and concocted a story that she
was just buying the ticket for Mom,
and they believed it.

93

She'd brought Jeff onto the train with her, inside a duffel bag. Somewhere in Nevada, Jeff had wiggled his legs through the zipper-- and this "walking duffel bag" freaked out all of the passengers as it made its way down the aisle. That's what led to Barrie getting questioned, and ultimately discovered that she was alone.

"I'm sorry you've felt so lonely," Mom said.

"And I'm sorry, too, Mom," I added, "for letting Barrie walk Jeff by herself."

"Well, hindsight is twenty-twenty," Mom replied.

"No, it's one," Barrie insisted.

We looked at her, confused.

"Twenty over twenty can be reduced to one."

"You really are one in a million, Barrie," Mom observed.

"That means that there are 7,436 people just like me, then."

The old Barrie was back. That's when we knew she'd be all right.

CHAPTER NINE,

or "THAT TIME WE WENT TO THE ARCADE"

"What are you doing here?" - MOM

Mom was at the grocery store when there was a knock on the door.

"I can't leave the apartment, Chuy," I hollered. "I gotta watch Barrie and Sumo."

Then, another knock. *Maybe he can't hear me,* I thought. I sighed and got off the couch.

When I opened the door, my jaw dropped to the floor.

It was Dad.

We stared at one another.

"Look at you," he remarked.

Since I didn't have a mirror, I

couldn't exactly do that.

It was good to see him, for the most part-- although I had mixed feelings that I wasn't going to be able to sort out right then and there.

"I was just in the neighborhood and thought I'd stop by," he verbalized.

I *think* it was a joke.

He stuck out his hand to shake.

"I got Mom's letter. I think she wanted me to visit," he noted.

"Mm-hmm. Well, we probably don't need to mention the letter to her."

"Why's that?"

I fumbled for an answer, until I was saved by--

"Dad!" Sumo ran to embrace Dad.

Then Barrie followed. Dad gave her a hug and kissed her on the head.

"You scared everyone by running away," he commented toward her. "I'm glad you wanted to see me, but you gotta let us know."

"I know."

"Where's Mom?" Dad questioned.

"She'll be back any minute," I replied.

"Can I come in?"

We led him over to the couch, then we bombarded him with questions.

"How'd you know where we live?" "How did you get here?" "Why are you here?"

He laughed.

Then the door opened-- it was Mom, and she was just as surprised as we were.

Actually, she was more surprised.

"What are you doing here?" she examined.

She probably forgot to add, "Great to see you," and stuff like that.

"I'm in town for work. The Reds are playing the Dodgers," he explained.

Her hand was on her hip.

"You couldn't tell me you were coming?" she asked.

"It was a last-minute thing, and I wasn't sure I could make it. I didn't want to let you guys down if it turned out I couldn't fit it in."

"Huh," she noted, folding her arms. It's never a good thing when she does that.

"Can we talk in the kitchen?"

"Sure," Dad answered, as he wrestled Sumo on the couch.

"I mean, *right now.*"

"Oh. Okay. Back in a minute, kids."

They had a discussion in the kitchen, one of those conversations where they were whispering intensely in hushed tones.

We looked at one another glumly. Not only were we about to get in trouble for the letters, it was going to crush our entire mission of getting the family together.

"Is Dad gonna mention the letters?" Sumo asked.

Barrie did some quick calculations before acknowledging, "The probability is 93.7%."

"Our days are numbered," I fretted.

"All days are numbered," Barrie replied. That's what calendars are for."

Dad returned to the living room, as Mom held up our letter-- our worst nightmare confirmed.

"What is *this*?" she demanded.

"Hmm. It, uh, appears to be a letter of some kind," I keenly observed.

"Yes. Do you want to explain it?"

"Not especially."

"We're going to talk about this," she threatened. "Not right now, but we will."

We nodded solemnly.

"Until then, guys, I've got an hour with you," said Dad. "Then I have to go."

Dad put his arms around us and polled, "Who wants to have some fun?"

"I do!" Sumo yelled excitedly.

Some questions aren't meant to be answered, but he hasn't mastered that life skill yet.

Dad walked us to his rental car, which meant that, for once, he wasn't driving a car with a hole in the roof or a broken steering wheel.

He took us to an arcade, which we appreciated because we never get to play video games. Also, it briefly took our minds away from our impending doom with Mom.

While we were there, we burned through a lot of tokens. Barrie won a huge stuffed animal by dominating an old pinball machine. She used her math wizardry to figure out the best angles to hit the ball.

I found myself alone with Dad.

"What are you thinking about?" he asked.

"Me? Ah, you don't want to know."

"Sure, I do, bud."

"You do?"

"Of course."

I didn't want to tell him I was thinking about comebacks for Keith from fourth grade, so I had to lie.

"Well, I was just wondering why they don't call it a teethbrush."

"That's what you were thinking about just now?"

"Mm-hm."

Dad shook his head incredulously, then tried a different path:

"How are you doing, son?"

"Okay, I guess."

"You can be honest. It's just us."

"All right."

"How is Los Angeles?"

"I don't think we belong."

"Why do you think that?"

"I got beat up," I shrugged.

It was the first thing that came to mind. I don't know why.

"Did you fight back?"

"I think so."

"You *think*?"

"I threw a right hook, sort of, like you taught me."

(I wasn't lying, entirely. I may have attempted a punch.)

"That's good."

"He got hurt a little, too."

"Yeah?"

"From my face hitting his fists."

"I raised you to stand up for yourself," he said. "To be a man."

"It's just that I'm not very good at it."

He cringed.

"Have you been using your typewriter?" he inquired. "I mean, besides writing fake letters from Mom."

"Not really."

I knew that if I'd told him I'd written some stuff, he'd want to read it and then say something nice out of obligation-- but he'd probably secretly think it was boring.

"Well, I hope you start using it sometime. I'd like to read your thoughts."

"Thoughts about what?"

"Anything. Sometimes the best way to deal with things is through writing. It can take a long time to sound like yourself. Miles Davis said that. But you'll find your voice."

I shoved my hands in my pockets.

"Listen, Mars," Dad continued. "I

103

haven't told anyone this. Not even Mom. But I'm thinking about taking a new job. It's a job any sportswriter would want. Pays well."

"That's good. I mean, right?"

"It's in Boston, though."

My heart sank.

"It'd be long hours, at least for a while, so I may not get to talk to you as much."

As much as what? I wondered. We were barely talking as it was.

"So, what do you think about that?" he asked.

What did I think? My first thought was, *I've spent all summer trying to come up with ways to help us become a family again, and what was he thinking about?*

He'd been thinking about a new job, a new city. For himself.

Why had I cared so much, if he didn't?

My jaw clenched.

There was so much I wanted to say,

but I didn't know where to begin. Or how to begin.

All I could muster was, "I don't know."

I immediately scolded myself for, once again, not having the courage to speak up.

"After I get established, I should be able to visit you guys more often," Dad noted.

He went on to say more words, but my mind was already racing. I was quiet the rest of the night, thinking about him going to Boston.

Later, Dad walked us back to our apartment.

"Mom, look what I got!" Sumo expressed, as he showed off some plastic army guys he won from the arcade.

"Well, that's nice."

"And we got ice cream!"

We all frowned at him. There are things he needs to learn.

"They're not supposed to be eating junk," Mom chastised Dad, who shrugged innocently.

"Want to see my room?" Sumo asked Dad.

"Next time," remarked Mom. "He's got to be leaving now."

"Next time," Dad agreed.

"When's the next time?" Sumo pressed.

Dad looked at Mom. I don't think either of them were prepared to answer that.

"We'll see," Mom answered.

Dad waved to Mom: "Thanks for letting me take them out. Sorry for coming unannounced."

We hugged Dad goodbye.

Well, to be more exact, Sumo and Barrie hugged Dad.

In my case, Dad hugged me, but I didn't really hug back-- I just kind of stood there.

That'll make my disapproval clear, I thought, knowing it'd do nothing of the sort.

He put his arm on my shoulder.

"Take care of your brother and sister, okay?" he requested.

"All right."

"Mom, too. She may be an adult, but she needs you."

"Have you told her about Boston?" I asked.

"When the time's right."

He winked, and walked out the door, heading in the general direction of his car.

He looked like he didn't know exactly where he was going.

I'd like to think it was because he didn't want to go.

I wanted to call out and ask him why he couldn't just stay the night.

And I wanted to ask him to not take that new job in Boston.

I didn't, of course.

But I wanted to.

Mom insisted on discussing the

letters with us. She was angry that we'd hid all of it from her. Mostly, though, she was hurt.

Lying to your parents and then covering it up doesn't normally turn out well, and it didn't here.

We should've known all along that these letters would never bring our family together-- in fact, it would do the opposite.

But when you're desperate, you don't see clearly.

And if it's true that making a mistake means you're human, it only proved we were particularly human.

CHAPTER TEN,

or "THAT TIME WE WENT TO THE IGLESIA"

"Life is hard." - SUMO

One day, Mom came home from work
in the middle of the day. There wasn't
anything unusual about that, because
she often came home for her lunch
break.

But this day was different. She
didn't say much, she played with her
food, and didn't seem to be in a rush.
She didn't even yell at us about
anything.

"Mom," I asked, "Don't you need to
get back?"

"What?" she responded, absently.

"Aren't you supposed to be at work
now?"

She stared out the window. After a
long wait, she finally said, "Bring

109

your brother and sister to the couch."

No! my mind screamed. *Not the couch!*

All bad talks happened on the couch. Put it this way: Mom never once gathered us on the couch to tell us that we were going for ice cream.

We waited nervously for Mom to deliver her news, whatever it might be. I had my suspicions.

"Is this about Dad? Is he taking a new job?" I asked.

"What? Why would you ask that?"

I could tell my question threw Mom off. I wanted to jump in a time machine and go backwards thirty seconds to undo that.

"Uh, no reason," I replied. "Just curious."

"I got laid off today," she stated.

"What's that mean?" quizzed Sumo.

"They got rid of my department."

"What does *that* mean?"

"I'm out of a job."

"I still don't know--"

"Sumo!" Barrie and I shouted in unison.

How could this happen? We moved all the way across the country for this job.

Don't panic. Don't panic, I told myself. I didn't want my mind to wander, because that would make things worse. Instead, I thought I'd give Mom an opportunity to reassure us.

"What are we going to do?" I explored.

"I'm going to eat potato chips and watch TV," Mom answered.

"Okay, but after that."

"A different bag of potato chips."

That didn't help. Then she went to her room and closed the door behind her.

I turned to Barrie and Sumo.

"We've got to do something."

"Like what?" pressed Sumo.

I sensed this was exactly the type of moment Mom and Dad had been telling me about. This was the time to step up, the time to shine, and I desperately wanted to do that-- for me, and for Barrie and Sumo.

This is the point in stories where the protagonist gets a sudden and brilliant idea. As the protagonist of this story, though, I definitely did not experience that.

"I'll think about it for a few days and get back to you," I finally concluded.

As far as inspirational movie speeches go, that would not crack the top ten.

Then, an unexpected thing happened. Sumo handed me a list he'd written.

It was a list of things he could do in the neighborhood to help bring in money for the family.

He was going to start a lemonade stand that he'd manage three days a week. He was going to mow lawns, walk other people's dogs, and wash cars.

Of course, he's terrible at all of those things. He'd get bored within seconds at a lemonade stand. He didn't know how to mow lawns. And we couldn't even get him to walk Jeff, let alone someone else's dog.

But none of that mattered. What *did* matter was that he showed, in a very simple way, that he wanted to help.

How was it that my little brother had the ability to just *do* things without even giving it much thought? And why didn't I have that gene?

I was supposed to be the leader, not him.

If I were to be honest, I'd have to acknowledge that I learned something from Sumo that day: sometimes, you don't need to spend so much energy thinking of that perfect thing to do or say. Sometimes, all you need to do is show someone that you care.

But I don't want to be honest, so I'll never say that-- especially not to him.

Mom was really touched by Sumo's list. And Sumo's thoughtful gesture turned out to be a theme for the rest of that summer: when there's a need, people around you often step up to help-- and it doesn't always come from places you expect.

A perfect illustration of unexpected support that summer was from a church that was only a block from our apartment. Chuy and his parents attended that church, and they invited us one Sunday.

I remember very clearly the first time we visited it. The building had a small sign that said, "Iglesia," which is Spanish for church. I never knew the actual name of the church.

It was much smaller than our old church in Ohio. It was the size of a living room, and there were no seats-- just rows of uncomfortable benches that hurt your butt after a while.

The pastor mostly spoke Spanish. In fact, we were the only non-Spanish speakers there. Everyone must've thought we entered by mistake.

I felt like at any moment, the pastor was going to point at us and say, "Get these people out of here."

Actually, for all we knew, he did say that-- since we had no idea what he was talking about.

Curiously, people loudly blurted

out things after the pastor declared
something. This really confused me. I
asked Mom what was going on, but she
shushed me.

"They're just agreeing with the
pastor," Chuy explained.

The music was really different,
too. Our church in Ohio had pipe
organs and a piano, violin and cello.
Here, it was one guy that played a
guitar while his wife sang loudly. Her
voice had a lot of "personality." It
was "unique" and "interesting."

Those are all ways of saying
her voice wasn't very good-- which I'd
never say...at least not to her.

The songs were sung in Spanish,
and everyone sang them
enthusiastically. Sumo felt right at
home. He clapped his hands and sang
loudly.

But when everyone sat down, I
noticed The Kid With the Orange Shirt
in the front row.

No! Not him!

What's he doing here? I
wondered. *How is it possible that my
luck is this bad?*

115

*And doesn't he ever wear
something besides that orange shirt?*

I felt him eyeing me, so I
looked down at the floor.

*He can't just walk over and beat
me up again, can he? Not in the middle
of church. That would be frowned upon,
right?*

It turned out that he was the
pastor's son. *Why can't he be more
like his father?* I contemplated. *It
would really help my situation if he
would listen to these sermons more
closely.*

The pastor inquired if anyone
wanted to share their testimony, which
is like their life story. Sumo raised
his hand.

Mom whispered, "No, Sumo!" I
punched him on the arm. But, of
course, the pastor called on him.

I ducked behind Chuy. I didn't
want anyone to know I was related to
Sumo, although that was impossible
because we were pretty easy to pick
out.

One look at Mom's furious face,
and I knew she wanted to storm out
right then.

"Life is hard," Sumo began.

"Ah," affirmed the pastor. "Tell us."

"Do you know what it's like to have an older brother and sister?"

The pastor translated Sumo's words into Spanish, as the congregation nodded.

"One time, my Mom got so mad at me for spilling food on the floor that she--"

"Disciplined!" Mom interjected.

As everyone turned their attention to her, she smiled politely and added, "In a calm, patient tone."

117

"Does that mean spanked?" Sumo contested. "Because I got spanked."

Mom's face turned red, and she sat back down. As the pastor translated, the people laughed.

Sumo continued, "I didn't even spill the food. My brother was the one who did it."

Everyone looked at me.

I went from wanting to leave a good impression to just wanting to leave.

From that point forward, Sumo was a celebrity in the church. As the summer wore on, he began copying everyone and blurting out things in Spanish, too.

Everyone loved that. Well, not Mom, Barrie or I-- we didn't care for it.

But everyone else did.

And I have to admit, I really appreciated the people at the church that summer. At a time when we really needed it, they treated us like family-- despite the fact that we didn't look like them or speak the same language.

Even the Kid With the Orange Shirt left me alone each Sunday. I wanted to believe it was because he'd noticed the effects on my biceps from that one time I did pushups in my room, but it probably was because he feared the wrath of his dad, or maybe God.

Either way, I was grateful that he allowed me safe passage.

CHAPTER ELEVEN,

or "THAT TIME WE WENT TO THE CIRCUS"

"I just wanted you guys to have a good time." — MOM

Saturday was the big day. We were looking forward to it all week.

Even though Mom was still searching for a new job and money was tight, she had purchased four tickets to a circus that was coming to town.

She wanted to create some experiences together in our new city.

We'd been counting down the days, and finally it was here.

All of us kids woke up at sunrise as if it were Christmas morning. We jumped on Mom's bed and chanted, "Circus! Circus!"

This seemed to annoy Mom. I got the sense that she really just wanted

120

to sleep...mainly because she
screamed, "I just want to sleep!"

She threw a pillow at us. I'm
pretty sure it was intended for Sumo,
but he ducked, and it hit me right in
the face. Mom isn't always the most
subtle person, especially in the
morning.

After waiting for Mom for what
seemed like forever, we were finally
on our way.

You know the circuses you see in
movies, where there are massive
weightlifting guys from Russia named
Igor, and elephants that can tap-dance
on a thin rope high in the air? Well,
this was nothing like that. It didn't
even look as cool as the one we went
to back in Ohio.

There was a "ring of death,"
which was a circle of fire that you
walk through. With a name like that,
normally I'd start telling Mom what
songs I'd like to have played at my
funeral.

But then I saw the flames--
about six inches high-- and even I
couldn't find anything to worry about.

Barrie calculated the odds of us
actually dying at literally zero.

When we took our seats, we saw a lot of the other kids eating popcorn and cotton candy, which smelled incredible. Mom pointed a finger at us: "Don't even ask."

Before the various acts started, two clowns ran between the rows, squirting water guns at one another and throwing pies while goofy music played.

So, we can all agree that clowns are creepy, right? I mean, who is the person that thought, "I've got the perfect idea: a man dressed up in a red wig and big nose. But wait, it gets better. He's got huge shoes and white makeup. I know it seems like he's about to rob a bank, but his purpose is to make kids laugh. This will be great."

Then the real show began. We saw
a trainer walk out with a "terrifying
beast."

It was a lion, but it was kind
of small. Maybe it was a baby lion.
I'm not sure it was even a lion.

Either way, it wasn't following
its trainer's instructions. Rather
than roaring, it just kind of napped.
I think the trainer was embarrassed
because he started telling jokes and
making little balloon animals.

I thought, *If I wanted that,
I'll go to the booth where they make
balloon animals. At least that guy is
an expert.*

But that was before we went to
the balloon animal booth. When we did,
Sumo asked for a sword, which the guy
made in seconds. Sumo was so excited
to have a new weapon to jab me with.

I requested a dog, but he made
me a sword, too. I figured he didn't
hear me, but I didn't care enough to
ask him again.

Then Barrie pushed for a
giraffe-- but the guy just made
another sword. That's when we realized
that he only knew how to do one thing:
make swords.

123

On the drive home, things spun out of control. We complained about different aspects of the circus. There were lots of topics to choose from, so the complaining went on for a while.

Finally, Mom yelled as loud as she could-- which is a natural talent of hers, by the way-- and pulled the van to the side of the road.

We all knew to shut up, because it was a very good bet that the next part wasn't going to go well.

It didn't.

"I paid a lot of money for those tickets!" she yelled. I don't remember exactly what else she said, but veins

124

were popping out of her neck. She
threatened that we were all grounded
forever, until the end of time.

Barrie debated briefly with Mom
about the precise definition of when
time ended, but quickly realized it
was a losing effort.

When Mom finally stopped
yelling, she paused and then did that
thing where she tries stopping herself
from crying.

Her shoulders shook a little
bit, and then she got herself under
control. You could hear a pin drop.

(Although, I should point out,
no pin actually dropped. That would've
been weird. Why is that even a phrase,
anyway?)

"Your Dad is going to move to
Boston," Mom suddenly offered.

So, it's true, I thought. *He's
really going to move even further away
from us. If he could move to Boston,
why couldn't he move to Los Angeles?
None of this made sense to me.*

"Why would he do that?" Barrie
asked.

"He's taking a new job there."

"Can we move to Boston, too?"
asked Sumo.

"Listen," Mom started, "I know
things have been hard on you, with
your dad not being with us. That's why
I just wanted you guys to have a good
time today."

"We *did* have a good time,"
Barrie insisted.

"You did?"

We all nodded-- well, except
Sumo, but after I secretly smacked him
on the back of the head, he got with
the program.

"All you did was complain," Mom
stated.

"That's just what we do," Barrie
argued.

"It's what we're good at," I
added.

I didn't intend for it to be a
joke, but Mom laughed. Then so did
Barrie and Sumo.

Maybe it was one of those times
where you have to laugh so you don't
cry. It felt good to laugh, but
especially good to laugh *together*.

126

Mom told us her favorite part of the circus was the hayride. I thought the hayride was pretty lame, honestly, and I didn't even understand why a circus would have a hayride in the first place.

But she explained that she liked it because it reminded her of her very first date with Dad. I couldn't imagine how a hayride would be involved in a perfect first date, but that's what they did.

She recalled how, in the middle of that hayride, Dad stood up to sing her a few verses from a song. That was a story we'd never heard before.

She smiled as she told it, which I noticed-- because it was the first time in a long time that she smiled as she talked about him.

It made me think that if both of them spent more time remembering those moments together, even after everything that had happened...maybe there was still a chance they could get along.

And maybe someday we could be a family again.

CHAPTER TWELVE,

or "THAT TIME I GOT MOVIE TICKETS"

"Bro." - *CHUY*

     I was skateboarding in the pool with Izzie when the apartment manager asked if I'd look after his cat while he went out of town. In exchange, he gave me two movie passes. I don't like cats, but I do like movies.

     "What movie are you gonna see?" Izzie pried.

     "Oh, I don't know. Maybe... *Jungle Jim*," I answered, eyeing her hopefully.

     Jungle Jim was a new animated movie about a down-on-his-luck chimpanzee. It looked pretty funny.

    "Do you, y'know..." I began.

    "What?"

    "Wanna see it?"

"Me?" she shrugged. "Nah."

But moments later, she added, "Well, maybe."

A sliver of hope!

"Oh. Because, you know, if you wanted. I mean, whatever."

Now that I've made myself very clear, I thought, *the ball's in her court.*

"Doesn't Chuy want to see it?"

"Chuy?" I replied innocently.

Let me hit pause on this for a second to mention a few small details.

All summer, Chuy had talked about *Jungle Jim.* He made me watch the trailer a dozen times.

So, sure, Chuy would've been the "obvious" person to invite. And, yes, he "desperately wanted to see the movie," and I guess you could say he "deserved it more than anyone."

On the other hand, I thought, *Izzie is here right now. It'd be rude not to ask her, wouldn't it?*

The truth was, I saw an opportunity to go to a movie with Izzie, and I was simply trying to justify it.

"I think he's gonna see it with another friend," I finally suggested.

I *thought* I'd heard him say something like that. Maybe. It's possible, at least.

Okay, fine. It was a complete lie.

"Huh," she responded.

That means she wants to see the movie with me, right? I thought.

We skated in the pool a little while longer. As we finished up and said our goodbyes, I asked her, "So, what time?"

She looked confused.

"Which movie screening tomorrow?" I clarified.

"Oh. You want me to go with you?"

"Yeah. I mean, I thought..."

*How could she not have
understood what we'd already talked
about?*

"But either way," I concluded.

"All right. Whatever. I'll go,"
she responded. "Maybe the afternoon."

"Cool."

I lay in bed that night,
replaying her words in my head: "All
right. Whatever. I'll go."

*Did that mean she really wants
to go, and she was just playing it
cool? Or is she only going because I
made her feel guilty?*

I spent most of the next day
nervously walking around the house and
adjusting drawers.

I casually told Mom I was going
to the movies, since I had a free
ticket.

"Who are you going with?"

"You know Izzie, right?"

"Yeah."

I opened and closed another
drawer, hoping she'd drop the subject.

No such luck.

"Who else?" she pushed.

"What do you mean?"

"Is anyone else joining you?"

"Like who?"

"Chuy, for example."

"No, he couldn't go."

"So, it's just you and Izzie?"

"If you want to put it like that."

"Is there another way to put it?"

"I guess not."

"Mars, stop fiddling with the drawer."

"Okay."

"Is this a date?"

"A date? No, I mean...why would...?"

"What would Izzie call it?"

"I think she'd call it two
people watching a movie. For free."

She nodded, finally letting it
go. But I could feel her eyes watching
me closely.

I stared at myself in the
bathroom mirror and brushed my hair.
This was where you're probably
supposed to put shaving cream on your
face, like Dad would do, but I didn't
have any peach fuzz on my face to
shave.

Finally, I left the apartment
and knocked on Izzie's door. She was
dressed in her usual sweatshirt.

I was hoping she'd be wearing
something special, because that would
indicate how she felt about me. *That's
just her style*, I told myself.

We walked to the movie theater
down the street. I saw my Mom
following us, pretending she had a
sudden need to buy a newspaper from
the newsstand on the street corner,
but I wasn't fooled.

We arrived at the theater early,
so the line wasn't long. We exchanged
our passes for movie tickets.

133

Since we had time to kill, we walked to the diner next to the movie theater.

The diner had a flashing sign, stating: "Now serving breakfast, lunch and dinner." I thought they might save themselves some space if the sign just said, "All the meals," but what do I know?

We decided to get a milkshake.

"I've got this," I said, shoving a pile of coins onto the counter. I had no idea if it was enough, but I knew I wouldn't be able to count while everyone stared at me-- it was too much pressure.

"You're 42 cents short," the hostess informed me, as she smacked her gum.

I motioned to Izzie it was no problem as I frantically dug through my pockets.

But it was as pointless as opening the refrigerator in hopes that there's a tasty snack you hadn't noticed before.

I felt my face turn bright red.

Unless the hostess was willing to take my library card for the rest of the payment, I was going to be out of luck.

Finally, Izzie handed the waitress a dollar.

This moviegoing experience was not off to a good start. We sat quietly as I desperately thought of something to say.

"Um, so if someone made fun of my name by asking what planet I was from, do you think it'd be a good comeback if I said, 'I'm from the planet where you need to give me more space'?"

"I don't get it."

"Space has to do with planets, but there's, like, two different meanings. I thought it was kind of clever. Maybe."

"I think you'd get beat up."

I mentally crossed it off the list of possible comebacks.

To break the awkwardness, she came to the rescue with her own "ice-breaker" question.

"If you could have dinner with anyone, dead or alive, who would it be?"

I mentally scrolled through a list of dozens of people: George Washington, Benjamin Franklin, the guy who invented Fat Free Potato Chips-- just so I could ask him what he was thinking.

The answer I went with was, "Definitely someone alive."

"You look distracted," she said. "It always looks like you're thinking."

"I don't mean to. I actually spend a lot of time thinking about ways to *not* look like I'm thinking so much."

"Mars? You're weird."

"Yeah. Probably."

When we entered the lobby of the theater, Chuy and a few other kids happened to pass by on their skateboards.

I turned my back and hoped Chuy wouldn't notice, but he saw us through the glass doors.

"Hey!" he greeted cheerfully, as he lightly banged on the door.

Izzie waved. I turned around to face him. *This was not going to be good.*

"What are you guys up to?" he asked.

I shrugged and pointed to the movie poster.

"You're watching *Jungle Jim*?"

"Yep."

"How'd you score tickets?"

"You know. The free tickets."

"You didn't tell me about it."

"Huh. I could've sworn I did."

I was sweating by then.

"He didn't invite you?" Izzie quizzed Chuy.

He shook his head. Then he shook his inhaler, brought it to his mouth, and skated away.

I wanted to say something, but I was left grasping for words, wrapped in guilt.

Izzie's eyes shot darts at me.

"I thought I'd talked to him about it," I mumbled.

She handed me her ticket.

"But this is yours!" I called out.

"Do whatever you want with it."

"Where are you going?"

"To talk to Chuy."

There I was-- standing by myself with two tickets to *Jungle Jim.*

I had no manual to tell me what to do in this situation, so I did what I usually did: I stared at the floor for a while.

I wanted to speak to the lady at the counter to see if I could exchange my tickets for future passes, but I was too embarrassed to do that.

I figured I should watch the movie so it wasn't a complete waste of the tickets. Besides, I didn't want my mom asking questions about why I was back so soon.

When I wandered into the theater, the movie had already begun. I could only find one empty seat. Of course, it was in the very first row.

I sat down and cocked my head to the side to see the screen.

I had a hard time deciding what was more irritating: the two kids who kept giving away what was going to happen next, or the crying baby next to me.

It was a tie.

I couldn't focus, anyway. All I could think about was the fact that I only had two friends in Los Angeles, and I'd just blown it with both of them.

That evening, I had a lot on my mind, so I took my little skateboard to the pool to practice a simple trick-- really the only one I knew.

It turned out that Chuy had the same idea. He was in the middle of the dimly lit pool, working on a spin move.

We looked at one another in uncomfortable silence.

I know Superman can stop trains in their tracks and throw actual buildings, but I think in this case, even he would've been, like, "You know what, guys? This situation here is just too heavy."

Finally, Chuy spoke:

"Bro."

It was neither a question nor the beginning of a sentence-- just a statement. The word hung in the air like a lead balloon.

This was one of the few times where he didn't have much to say.

"I wanted to see that movie," he mumbled.

"I know."

"You should've at least told me you'd rather go with Izzie."

140

I thought about all the times
Chuy stuck up for me during that
summer, even when it made him look
bad. Like when I got beat up, or when
I lost the boogie board he'd lent me.

The one chance I had to return
the favor with a movie ticket that
didn't cost me anything, I chose to
take Izzie instead.

"I'm sorry, Chuy. I didn't even
finish the movie."

"Was it a date?"

"Why is everyone asking that?"

"Kinda seemed like a date, bro."

"No. Definitely not a date."

Then I paused. I owed him
honesty.

"Maybe I wanted it to be," I admitted, "but it didn't end up that way."

"What do you mean?"

"When Izzie found out I didn't offer you the ticket first, she wasn't happy."

"She looks out for me."

"It's probably for the best, anyway," I shrugged.

"Girls, huh?" he offered, with a smile.

"Girls," I confirmed, and I was completely certain that neither one of us knew what we were talking about.

We shared a chuckle.

"So, I'll see you around, then," I said, with hope. It was really a question.

"Yeah, bro. See you around."

He nodded and took out his inhaler, and I think he somehow breathed life back into me.

CHAPTER THIRTEEN,

or "THAT TIME WE REDISCOVERED OUR
CULTURE"

"This is part of growing up, Mars." -
MOM

"Turning thirteen is great,"
they said. "Best time of your life,"
they said. "At that age, anything's
possible if you just imagine it," they
said.

It was a Friday when I turned
thirteen, and if there was one thing I
knew, it was that I didn't feel like
anything was possible if I just
imagined it.

I could tell that Mom really
wanted to cheer me up.

"I'm taking you to Chinatown on
your special day," she declared.
"Isn't that exciting?"

I appreciated the effort, but
'exciting' wasn't the first word that
came to mind.

143

She sensed that.

"It'll be good to explore your Chinese roots."

"We're only half," Barrie corrected.

"Fine. Half. But it's important to rediscover your culture."

"Rediscover? We never discovered it in the first place," I insisted. "Ohio isn't exactly China."

"Well, it's important that you feel more connected to it."

Mom is Chinese and had emigrated from Laos as a child, though she hadn't ever put much emphasis on that. But since we moved to Los Angeles, she'd begun encouraging us to learn more about our heritage.

Sumo grumbled. I felt like this surprise trip was more for Mom than it was to celebrate my birthday, but I was smart enough not to suggest that.

When we first entered Chinatown, we were greeted by a "Dragons Gate" entrance, in case it wasn't already obvious where we were by the millions of Chinese signs.

We approached a large statue of a Chinese man sitting on a chair. It looked like he was deep in thought.

"Who's this supposed to be?" I asked.

"This was an important revolutionary who helped lead the fight," Mom replied.

"What fight?"

"The fight. You know, the fight."

"What was his name?"

"It's very difficult to pronounce."

"You don't know who he is, do you?" Barrie observed.

"Look," Mom admitted, "I'm sure he was a great man."

We tossed coins into a wishing well, and we entered a temple-- until Sumo made too much noise and got us kicked out.

There was a small museum where we learned about the history of Chinese people in the West, and the troubles they faced. From what I gathered, they were taken advantage of.

"Isn't that shocking?" Mom asked.

Shocking? I recalled the books I'd read about the Thanksgiving story-- the real story-- and about our nation's history with, you know, the buying and selling of humans. Slavery and whatnot.

So, just hear me out, but no-- this didn't seem especially shocking.

We walked through a flea market where people were selling all kinds of things. If you ever needed to buy dried fish, a cheap umbrella, and a sweatshirt that says "Los Angles" (yes, that's a misspelling) all in one place, then you'd be in luck.

"Doesn't this make you feel more in touch with your culture?" asked Mom.

It did not, particularly, but I didn't want to discourage her.

Besides, I was occupied with wondering when Dad was going to call. It was the afternoon, and he still hadn't wished me a happy birthday. My disappointment was turning into resentment.

As we walked around the city, I thought about how Dad had prioritized a new job over us. And the drinking problem that he'd never even brought up with me.

I kept thinking about it when we got home.

"You look miserable, Mars," Mom observed. "Why don't you call him?"

It didn't seem like I should have to do that, but Mom persisted.

"You're not going to be able to stop thinking about it until you do it," she said.

I paced my room, considering what to say.

Mom knew I'd be doing this too.

She knocked on my bedroom door, and hollered through the wall.

"Just say exactly what's on your mind."

"I don't know what's on my mind."

"Say it anyway. Just be honest. Be yourself."

Be yourself? I thought. *What an awful idea. That's the last thing I want.*

"This is part of growing up, Mars," she continued. "He needs to hear what you're feeling."

I paced some more, then I laid on my bed for a while.

Why am I spending so much time thinking about what to say? I admonished myself. *He isn't going to pick up the phone, anyway.*

Except that he did.

After I suddenly dialed his number, he surprised me by answering right away.

"Hey, bud," he greeted.

He sounded more joyful than I felt.

"Dad, you didn't, um...you didn't call me today."

148

There was a brief pause. I could picture him realizing it was my birthday.

"I was just about to call you, Mars."

"You were?"

I wanted to believe him, but there was another pause.

"No. I'm sorry. The truth is, I forgot."

In that moment, something shattered inside of me. I think it was hope.

"It's once a year, Dad."

"This is no excuse," he began, before promptly giving one.

He explained how he was distracted with writing deadlines, and that he was in the middle of packing for Boston.

Maybe it was that I had just become a teenager, or perhaps I was sick of not having the courage to say how I felt. Or it may have been a combination of both.

Either way, without even thinking

about it, I expressed what I felt, as
I felt it, for the very first time.

"I don't care about your reasons,"
I stated defiantly. "I don't deserve
this."

"You're right, son. You don't."

"I know about your problem, you
know."

"Problem?"

"With drinking. Mom told me."

There was stunned silence on his
side. Then he finally answered.

"I'm getting help, Mars. Every day
I'm beating it. And I'll continue to
beat it. That's my promise to you."

"I hope you do. But I don't want
to talk to you anymore."

"I understand. I'll call you
tomorrow."

"No," I replied, surprising
myself. "Not tomorrow, or the next
day. Not until *I've* decided I want to
talk to you again."

As I hung up, I knew immediately
that, good or bad, there were some

things that would never be the same between us.

In some ways, I was proud that I stood up for myself, even if it was against Dad.

But I was wrestling with doubt.

Had I just destroyed any chance that our family would be happy and together again?

Mom came in my room.

"I heard some of that conversation," she said.

I looked down at the floor, embarrassed.

"I want you to know I'm proud of you. That took real courage."

My eyes looked up briefly.

"Sometimes, you have to tell people things they don't want to hear," she continued. "All you can do is be honest. You can't control how they react to it. He needs to know that he's let you down."

"What if he won't talk to me anymore?"

151

"He'll always want a good relationship with you, Mars."

"How do you know that?"

"He's a good man. Don't forget that."

Was he a good man? I didn't know anymore.

I stared at the typewriter in my room. It reminded me of the letters that got us into trouble. And it reminded me of the sportswriting job Dad had chosen over us.

I suddenly hated it.

I kicked it.

That was a poor choice-- because I almost broke my toe. I'd forgotten how heavy it was.

But I got my revenge.

I marched that typewriter to the parking lot and heaved it in the orange dumpster.

When I woke up the next day, I decided I shouldn't have done that. I rummaged through the dumpster.

But it was gone.

CHAPTER FOURTEEN,

or "THAT TIME I HEARD A MARIACHI BAND"

"That's just Jeff's love language."

- MOM

It was the day after my birthday--
the day that the small party I'd
planned was supposed to happen.

I had invited Chuy and Izzie and
a couple of other kids from the
apartment complex. Unfortunately, the
Kid With the Orange Shirt informed me
that he was coming when he overheard
me talking about it.

I think he just wanted to eat
some free hamburgers, but I couldn't
say no-- otherwise, he might get all
beat-up-ish toward me.

That morning, Jeff decided to
leave me a special gift that only he
could-- by pooping in the middle of my
floor.

I didn't know it yet, but that was an indication of things to come.

I got a package in the mail from Aunt Sarah, my dad's sister. She always sent random, homemade gifts that were not useful in any way. Once again, she didn't disappoint.

Buried deep inside the package was some kind of clay piece she'd made. It was lumpy and slanted, and had a handle that was already broken.

"Make sure to write her a thank-you letter," Mom lectured.

"What do I call this thing?"

"It's a container, obviously. No, wait-- it's a jar."

We finally settled on calling it a mug, so I wrote a letter to Aunt Sarah, describing my "passion" for the new mug.

The game plan for my party was to celebrate at the park. Mom was going to grill hamburgers and hotdogs while we ran around and "did stuff." (We hadn't really defined "stuff" at that point.)

We were to meet at my place at noon, but when the clock struck twelve and no one arrived, I started to worry.

"They'll be here soon. They're just running late," Mom stressed.

She's probably right, I figured. *They must've lost track of time.*

Although, I thought, *it's not like Chuy to be late. Or Izzie, for that matter. Maybe they're sending a message. Maybe they're still angry about the movie ticket thing, and they're boycotting my birthday.*

What if they protest my birthday, and they make signs, and they get a crowd to march in a circle around the apartment complex? What if they lead a movement that sweeps the nation, like the documentary I saw about the Vietnam War? What then?

I headed to Chuy's apartment, but he wasn't there.

I went to Izzie's. Same result.

This is it, I thought to myself. *I'll have to change my name and move to some island, where I'll have to hunt for food-- and the extent of my hunting experience is looking for hard-to-find snacks buried deep in the cupboard.*

A couple of kids finally
arrived, including the Kid With the
Orange Shirt-- which was really
uncomfortable-- but still no Chuy or
Izzie.

Mom walked us to the park. I
knew she was trying, and she meant
well, but all of this only reminded me
that Dad wasn't here. That Chuy and
Izzie weren't here.

This was not how I envisioned my
party going. Or my summer, for that
matter.

If I were back in Ohio, I
thought, *I'd have a huge party with
all my good friends. Well, friends
that I liked. Or knew, at least.*

*Here, I have no real friends.
This can't get any worse.*

As a matter of fact, though,
things could get worse. I know this
now.

My mom looked at the Kid With
the Orange Shirt and said, "Mars,
aren't you going to introduce me to
your friend?"

"What? Um. Yeah," I sputtered.

It hit me that I still didn't know what his name was.

"He lives near Chuy," I continued. "I think. Right? So. Uh."

I mumbled for what felt like an hour. I tried everything except breakdancing to change the subject-- and if I knew how to breakdance, I'd have done that, too.

Suddenly, though, the Kid With the Orange Shirt ended my embarrassment with one statement.

"I don't have a lot of friends," he told my mom, as he looked down at the ground, "but Mars is a good friend."

I was stunned.

I later found out that he appreciated me not telling his dad, the pastor, that he'd beaten me up-- but he'd just never communicated that.

To be clear, I still had no clue what his name was, but at least that was something to build on.

Mom passed out the cupcakes she brought. We began to sing Happy Birthday the only way we knew how...badly out of tune. Well, except

the Kid with the Orange Shirt-- he did
not appear to sing at all.

Then I heard musical instruments
approaching, loudly joining in. I
turned around.

It was Chuy playing the trumpet,
and Izzie playing the guitar.

They were dressed up as if they
were a Mariachi band. Chuy wore a huge
black sombrero with a matching outfit
that made him look like a sparkly
cowboy.

Izzie had a red flower in her
hair. It was a good look for her--
even if it wasn't her style.

Chuy didn't sound like he'd ever
played trumpet before. He concluded
the song with the horn right in my
face, blowing my hair back.

I was so relieved to see them...
especially Izzie, because I hadn't
spoken with her since the Movie
Theater Incident.

"I didn't know you guys could
play," I commented.

"We can't," Chuy responded
cheerfully.

At least he knows, I thought.

"Sorry we're late," he remarked.
"We had to get these costumes from my
uncle to celebrate your birthday in
style."

"I'm just glad you're here."

I brought Izzie a cupcake.

"Hey," I said.

159

Her response was equally riveting.

"Hey."

After that profound exchange, I was confident our friendship would return to normal.

She and Chuy gave me a birthday gift: a skateboard. They had traded with another kid to get it, and it immediately became the coolest thing I owned.

Even the Kid With the Orange Shirt gave me something. Well, two things. Granted, the first was a punch on the shoulder that left a bruise for a week-- but I do feel like it was heart-felt, so that was cool.

The second thing he gave me, though, was Dad's old typewriter.

It turned out he'd seen me toss it in the dumpster and figured I'd want it back, so he brought it to his apartment and cleaned it up.

Later that evening, Barrie gave me her gift: a book about the electromagnetic spectrum, which was cool-- although not as cool as, say, a basketball. Or really anything else.

Sumo got me a remote control for a TV that we didn't own. I didn't know what that was all about, but at least *he* was excited about his gift.

Mom gave me a new chess board with all the pieces. That made me think of Dad, because he had taught me to play. I wished he could've been with us.

Before we went to bed, Jeff left another dump on the floor for me to clean. That was his way of interacting with me.

"That's just Jeff's love language," Mom explained.

"I wish he could learn to express his love in a different way," I replied.

"Look at it like this, Mars," said Barrie positively. "If the success of a birthday could be measured by the amount of dog poop you had to clean, then it was a really good day."

I don't know why anyone would measure success that way, but if you did, then she was right.

CHAPTER FIFTEEN,

or "THAT TIME WE WENT FOR PIZZA"

"Subjectively, I'd have to say I think...um, feel...positive about it."
- BARRIE

Right before I was to start junior high, I received an envelope in the mail from the school. It was my class schedule.

I stared at it. Things were getting real.

In two days, I'll be wandering the junior high hallways, holding my schedule and looking for my classes. This is the big time.

Everyone will know I'm new. I might as well be a tourist with a map.

I realized that I needed to write a list of comebacks so that if anyone made fun of me, I'd have one ready for any situation.

Which reminded me, I still didn't
even have one for Keith from the
fourth grade.

There was a knock on my door.

"Mars! I got my class schedule!
Mars!" shouted Chuy, as he pounded on
the door.

I let him in.

"Where's your schedule?" he
investigated.

It was sitting on the coffee
table, untouched.

"Open it! We gotta see if we're in
any of the same classes," he insisted.

He ripped it open before I could
even get a look at it.

"Bro, look at your fifth period,"
he blurted. "Pottery?"

"That's my elective," I explained.

"Was the cross-stitching class all
filled up?" he laughed.

"Well, what's *your* elective?" I
challenged.

"Woodworking."

I scoffed-- "Who do you think you are, Paul Bunyan?"

"You mean the legendary lumberjack with superhuman strength?"

Bad example, I scolded myself. *Once again, my comeback was not well thought-out.*

I knew I'd land on the losing end of this debate. Luckily, Barrie came to my defense.

"The question isn't which class is cooler. Empirically, they're equally un-cool," she stated. "The real question is, which class is easier to earn an 'A'? Data says it's pottery."

"See?" I pointed. "She gets it."

The good news was, it looked like Chuy and I would be in the same P.E. class. It somehow made me feel better that if the P.E. teacher was going to scream at me for running slow laps around the track, at least I knew I'd be faster than Chuy.

When Mom got home from work that evening, she implored us to all sit down on the couch.

ON THE COUCH?!! NOOOOOOO!

She must've sensed our panic,
because she inserted, "Don't worry,
it's not bad. It's just a favor. Would
the three of you be willing to help
our new neighbor?"

"Can we answer truthfully?" Barrie
contested.

We all laughed at the absurdity of
Barrie's question.

"Yeah...no," replied Mom, still
chuckling.

"What do they need?" I sighed.

"Help moving furniture into their
apartment."

We groaned.

"What are *you* going to be doing,
Mom?" I protested.

"I'll be overseeing you."

I can't wait to be an adult so I
can just oversee my kids while they do
all the work.

"Who are these new neighbors?" I
asked.

"You'll have to meet them."

"I just hope they don't play music loudly."

"I hope they're not annoying," Sumo chimed in.

"Or frivolously ignorant," added Barrie.

"Do you really think *we're* not all of those things?" Mom responded. "People who live in glass houses shouldn't throw stones."

"Why would people live in glass houses?" questioned Sumo.

"Technically," added Barrie, "if you live in any form of non-crystalline amorphous solid, you shouldn't throw anything at all."

We knocked on the neighbor's door, but no one answered.

"Oh, well," I said. "At least we tried."

I tip-toed toward our apartment, but I knew we wouldn't get off that easy. Mom made us sit around and wait.

Eventually, we saw the legs and arms of a man carrying a tall stack of boxes.

"Maybe that's him," Mom theorized.

I sighed and approached the man.

"Uh, excuse me. Need a hand?"

"No, thanks," he grunted, before setting down the boxes.

That's when we saw who the new neighbor was.

It was Dad.

"But I'll take a hug," he added.

We stared at him, stunned.

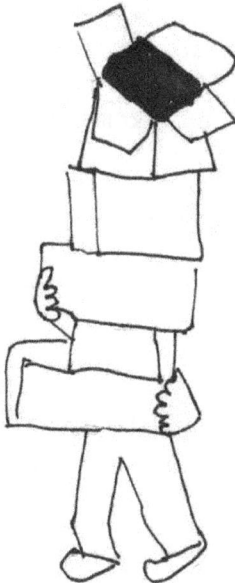

"I thought that might get a bigger reaction. No?" he continued.

We looked at Mom, who shrugged.

She was in on it.

After our shock wore off, I said, "I thought you moved to Boston?"

"I decided against it in the end."

"Why?"

"Well," he said, as he put his hand on my shoulder, "someone made me realize that I couldn't."

Then it hit me.

He had listened to me. Our phone conversation had affected him. Perhaps it had paid off to speak my mind, after all.

"You're really going to live in the apartment next door?" Barrie asked.

"Yup."

"But not in our apartment?"

"Nope."

"Why not?"

"Someday soon, maybe."

Dad took all of us out for pizza, even Mom. Of course, the drive there was quite an experience.

His latest car was huge. It looked like a boat-- and didn't even drive as well as one. The seats had rug-like material that was thumbtacked to keep it together.

We noticed that the heater was on full-blast. Since it was still summertime, this was not ideal.

We pressed Dad to kindly turn it off.

"It doesn't really like to be shut off."

For our sake, he tried-- but it made a strange churning noise before belching out a puff of dust, then continued to blast hot air.

"Just roll down the windows," he sighed.

Mom shook her head, but bit her tongue. For her, that took some facial gymnastics.

We eventually got to the restaurant alive, at which point we dug into the piping hot pizza like a pack of ravenous dogs.

Dad leaned forward: "So, guys, what do you think?"

"What do I think?" wondered Barrie. "We should've gotten yellow and red peppers. The pairing is not only pleasing to the eye, aesthetically, but the variety in taste complements the sausage."

Dad took a moment to process.

"No, I mean about me moving next door," he clarified.

"Oh. Well, I imagine that it makes the passing of information more efficient."

"Feelings, Barrie. How do you *feel*?"

"Subjectively, I'd have to say I think...um, feel...positive about it."

"I think it's great!" Sumo interjected. "You can take us out to ice cream and stuff!"

"No," Mom corrected. "He'll be helping you with your homework."

"Maybe a little of both, if you

play your cards right," Dad suggested.

He turned to me: "How 'bout you, bud?"

I took a deep breath.

"I'd have to say I agree with Barrie about the yellow and red peppers."

"See?" Barrie affirmed.

Dad frowned.

"But I guess it makes me feel..."

I paused to think of a word that captured what I wanted to say.

Dad waited, listening carefully.

"Happy," I concluded.

"Happy," he repeated. "Happy is good. I'm happy you're happy."

As we ate, Dad informed us that he got a new job writing for a website in Los Angeles, and that he was also going to write for a nearby minor league baseball team.

"You're going from the major leagues to the minors...*on purpose*?" I pried.

"To me, it's the other way around. Sometimes life is like that."

He explained that the letters we wrote to him initially caused an argument between he and Mom, but wound up sparking conversation between them.

Those conversations led to the possibility of repairing things.

"I knew I needed to find a way to get here," he determined. "Whatever it took."

Later that night, Mom and Dad went for a walk.

We folded open the apartment blinds slightly because we didn't want them to know we were spying.

"Look!" shouted Sumo. "They're holding hands."

"No, they're just in close proximity," Barrie observed.

I angled myself for a better view. It was dark and I couldn't really tell for sure, but the main thing was that they were near each other, and seemed to be getting along.

Something changed that night. We all felt it.

172

We began to allow ourselves to dream again, to think that maybe we could stitch the family back together the way it should've always been.

That made me feel like hugging Barrie and Sumo, and never letting them go.

I mean, I didn't do that...because that would've been unpleasant for all involved.

Instead, I settled for watching Barrie judge Sumo's somersaults on the couch.

But I had a smile on my face that couldn't be wiped off.

"Guys," I exclaimed, "here's what we're going to do. When they come back, we'll tell Dad we're glad he moved to Los Angeles."

"He already knows," said Sumo.

"We'll tell him anyway."

They actually listened to me.

And when we told him that, I'm pretty sure a tear formed in his eye.

"Is someone chopping onions over there?" he asked, with a smile.

We surrounded both Mom and Dad. I think it was to make sure this was all still real.

"Well, guys, it's getting late. I've got to begin the long journey back to my place," he joked.

"Hey Dad, can you sing the song that you sang to Mom?" asked Sumo.

"What song is that?"

"On the hayride? When you had your first date?"

Dad looked at Mom: "You told them about that?"

She nodded.

"How about tomorrow, okay?" he said, patting Sumo on the head. "It's pretty late."

That seemed reasonable. We hugged him goodnight, and then he pulled me aside.

"Mars, I want to thank you."

"For what?"

"For sticking with me. For telling me how you felt. For showing me that I needed to fight for my family. For

leading Barrie and Sumo. And most of
all, for being you. You're enough,
just the way you are."

I'd never heard him say anything
like that to me. I was floating in
air.

Not literally, of course, because
science. But that's how it felt.

I began to get the odd feeling
that everything might turn out okay.

That was not normal for me.

Who knows? I thought. *Maybe even
junior high was going to be all right.*

And somewhere along the way, I no
longer felt the need to come up with
that perfect comeback for Keith
anymore.

About the authors:

SETH LARSEN was born at an early age. Legendary jazz man, award-winning documentarian, avid unicyclist: he is none of those things. Seth is currently tolerated by his wife, Jacqueline, and their four children in La Cañada, CA. **DAYLEN** and **KAI LARSEN** are twin sixth graders at Paradise Canyon Elementary. Daylen likes to gather his siblings and tell stories about what life was like back when he was Kai's age, two minutes ago. Kai still puts his pants on one leg at a time, just like everyone else—not because he's humble; it's just because he's unclear how else you'd go about it.

SETH "SUMO" LARSEN is in the fourth grade. He does not particularly like to draw, and only did so here because he was promised an extra helping of dessert. He is best described as a piece of work. **SAVAHN "SHIU SHIU" LARSEN**, on the other hand, loves art. She's a creative third grader who once accidentally fell down the stairs and drew a Picasso.